SOCIAL POLICY STUDIES NO. 20

University of
Hertfordshire

AGEING

IN

OECD COUNTRIES

A Critical Policy Challenge

ORGANISATION FOR ECONOMIC CO-OPERATION AND DEVELOPMENT

ORGANISATION FOR ECONOMIC CO-OPERATION AND DEVELOPMENT

Pursuant to Article 1 of the Convention signed in Paris on 14th December 1960, and which came into force on 30th September 1961, the Organisation for Economic Co-operation and Development (OECD) shall promote policies designed:

- to achieve the highest sustainable economic growth and employment and a rising standard of living in Member countries, while maintaining financial stability, and thus to contribute to the development of the world economy;
- to contribute to sound economic expansion in Member as well as non-member countries in the process of economic development; and
- to contribute to the expansion of world trade on a multilateral, non-discriminatory basis in accordance with international obligations.

The original Member countries of the OECD are Austria, Belgium, Canada, Denmark, France, Germany, Greece, Iceland, Ireland, Italy, Luxembourg, the Netherlands, Norway, Portugal, Spain, Sweden, Switzerland, Turkey, the United Kingdom and the United States. The following countries became Members subsequently through accession at the dates indicated hereafter: Japan (28th April 1964), Finland (28th January 1969), Australia (7th June 1971), New Zealand (29th May 1973), Mexico (18th May 1994), the Czech Republic (21st December 1995) and Hungary (7th May 1996). The Commission of the European Communities takes part in the work of the OECD (Article 13 of the OECD Convention).

Publié en français sous le titre :

LE VIEILLISSEMENT DANS LES PAYS DE L'OCDE

Reprinted 1997

FOREWORD

People in OECD countries are living longer. There are more people in older age groups and patterns of learning, work, leisure, care-giving and care-receiving over the course of life are changing. These trends pose fundamental challenges for fiscal, economic and social policies of OECD Member countries. Responding to these challenges requires a policy framework that integrates many areas of social and economic policy and squarely addresses ageing, life-course and inter-generational issues.

This report reviews the effects of ageing on pensions, health and long-term care, and the labour market, as well as its broader fiscal effects and its effects on the capital market. Three types of ageing are reviewed: *individual ageing* (people are living longer); *population ageing* (there are more people in older age groups as a consequence of the baby boom and baby bust); and *active ageing* (there are changes in patterns of activity within age groups – changes such as staying in school longer or retiring earlier). It is the combined effect of these three types of ageing which is of particular relevance to public policy. Analysis of individual ageing and population ageing is useful in identifying the challenges that demography poses for policy. The addition of active ageing considerably enriches that analysis and also points to possible solutions.

Ageing poses four main challenges for public policy. The first challenge is fiscal: in the absence of reform, ageing populations increase government spending, particularly on pensions. The second relates to market responsiveness: a framework is required within which labour and capital markets are able to respond quickly to the effects of ageing. The third suggests a more flexible allocation of time over the life-cycle. Flexible time allocation would reduce the need for government remedial actions in age groups that are growing in size, would ease fiscal pressures, and would lead to a healthier and more active population. The fourth challenge is to find a new balance between individual and collective responsibilities, particularly in pensions and dependent care.

These challenges require a coherent response. Without an overall strategy, there is a risk that reforms will pull in different directions. An appropriate reform strategy can also help build public support for needed reforms and overcome institutional barriers that exist in policy development and service delivery. That strategic response is needed now, not in a decade's time. The report reviews a range of fiscal, pension, labour market and health care reforms, and new directions for long-term care, that could be included in such a strategy.

The report was prepared by a team of OECD staff members, coordinated by Peter Hicks, formerly Senior Policy Advisor in Human Resource Development, Canada. It is published on the responsibility of the Secretary-General of the OECD.

TABLE OF CONTENTS

Chapter 1
Introduction and Overview

A. Introduction   9

B. Ageing populations and active ageing: a deepening of policy analysis   10

C. The effects of ageing   12
    Effects on individuals and families   12
    Effects on income and wealth   13
    Effects on the labour market and economy   14
    Effects on public policy   15
    Looking further ahead   15

D. Policy challenges and responses   15

E. Directions for reform   17
    Pensions   17
    Health and long-term care   22
    Labour market   23
    Fiscal effects, national saving and capital markets   23
    Need for early action   24

F. Proposals for Phase 2 of the study   25
    Core project   25
    Expanded level of activity   26

Chapter 2
Pensions

A. Overview   29

B. Responding to the fiscal challenge   31
    Fiscal scenarios for pension expenditures   31
    Incremental reform   40

C. Market responsiveness and active ageing challenges   47

D. Balancing individual and collective responsibilities   47

E. Conclusion: directions for reform   50

Chapter 3
Health and Long-term Care

A. Overview   51

B. Health care   52
    Age and health care consumption   52
    Difference among countries   53
    The importance of generational effects   56
    Health expectancy and future costs   56
    Reforms of health care systems   57

C. Long-term care   59
    Recent trends in long-term care policies   59
    Reforms in long-term care financing   61

D. Conclusion: directions for reform   63
    Research and development   63
    Prevention of illness and the promotion of health   63
    Education and training of health personnel   64
    Goals for long-term care   64

Chapter 4
Labour Markets

A. Overview   65

B. Reasons for low employment among older workers   68
    Factors affecting demand   68
    Factors affecting the willingness of older workers to participate in the labour market   72

C. The role of lifelong learning and active labour market policies   76

D. Conclusion: directions for reform   78

Chapter 5
Fiscal Effects, National Savings and Capital Markets

A. Overview   81

B. Overall fiscal scenarios   82

C. The revenue base   88

D. Financial market implications of ageing populations   92

E. Ageing and saving   93
    Effects of lower saving on living standards   97

F. Conclusion: directions for reform   97

Annex: Demographics   99
    Increasing dependency ratios   99
    Key assumptions underlying population projections 103

Notes   105

Bibliography   107

List of Tables

Table 1.1A.	Pensions, health and long-term care: possible directions for reform in light of the challenges posed by ageing populations	18
Table 1.1B.	Labour market, capital market, fiscal and other effects: possible directions for reform in light of the challenges posed by ageing populations	20
Table 2.1.	Standard age of entitlement to public pension in OECD countries, 1992 . . .	31
Table 2.2.	Net present value of pension contributions, expenditure and balances	36
Table 2.3.	Pension expenditures under various scenarios	38
Table 3.1.	Health expenditures by age group and standardisation of expenditure ratios	53
Table 3.2.	Concentration of total health expenditures on older people, 1993	54
Table 3.3.	Projected public health care costs in 2030	58
Table 4.1.	Percentage of the population in four age groups that had attained at least upper secondary education, 1992	77
Table 5.1.	Fiscal indicators, 1995 to 2030	83
Table 5.2.	Pure ageing effects on net financial liabilities, 2000-2030	88
Table 5.3.	Increase in tax/GDP ratios required to keep net debt constant	89
Table 5.4.	Structure of social security contributions, 1993	92
Table A.1.	Population indicators	100
Table A.2.	Population sub-groups	101
Table A.3.	Dependency and support ratios	102
Table A.4.	Key demographic factors	104

List of Charts

Chart 2.1.	Public pension payments and contributions	33
Chart 2.2.	Pension scenarios: variations from baseline	41
Chart 4.1.	Labour force participation rates for male workers aged 55 to 64	66
Chart 4.2a.	The fall in participation rates of male workers aged 55 to 64 and the rise in total unemployment rates, 1975-94	69
Chart 4.2b.	The fall in participation rates and the rise in unemployment rates of male workers aged 55 to 64, 1975-94	69
Chart 4.2c.	The fall in participation rates of male workers aged 55 to 64 and the rise in total male unemployment rates, 1975-94	70
Chart 4.2d.	The fall in participation rates of male workers aged 55 to 64 and the rise in youth unemployment rates, 1975-94	70
Chart 4.3.	Age profiles of average earnings	71
Chart 5.1.	Impact of different initial primary balances on net debt	85
Chart 5.2.	Demographic impact on future net national savings in OECD countries	96

Chapter 1

INTRODUCTION AND OVERVIEW

A. Introduction

In recent years, there has been much work in the OECD and elsewhere on the policy implications of ageing populations. The first purpose of this report is to summarise those findings. The second purpose is to propose an action plan for a possible second phase of this study that would enrich the quality of that policy advice. The study was launched following the May 1995 meeting of the OECD Council at Ministerial level. Ministers requested that the organisation "consolidate and analyse the policy implications of ageing populations with an initial report (...) by 1996".

An ageing perspective provides policy-makers with valuable insights on future challenges and potential directions. It is particularly powerful in understanding medium and longer-run challenges; demography is one of the few areas where it is possible to make meaningful projections that extend well into the next century. However, it is only a partial perspective. Ageing rarely operates in isolation from other forces of change – such as technology or trade. At any one time, these other factors are likely to be of even greater relevance to policy, but they cannot be projected more than a few years into the future. The report therefore examines alternative scenarios about the future and stresses the ways in which ageing may re-enforce or offset other trends.

A longer-term perspective does not mean that policy action can be postponed. In many countries, a window of opportunity exists in which to address both short- and long-term policy goals in ways that are mutually reinforcing. Further, unless action is taken soon, problems are likely to be much worse after 2010 in most Member countries as the heaviest effects of ageing populations begin to be felt.

This initial phase of the project is based on existing research on the policy implications of ageing. For example, more attention has been paid to public pensions, an area that has been well covered by OECD and other studies, and less attention to private pensions and capital markets. For similar reasons, more attention has been paid to older workers and less to other effects of ageing on the labour market. Nevertheless, in several areas, the report does include the results of new work. In particular, it has been possible to gain some new understanding of health care use by age in different countries, as well as of the fiscal implications of various reform strategies. A proposal for a second phase of the project outlines areas where there is likely to be high pay-off from further policy-oriented research and from study of the practical lessons learned as different countries have addressed the challenges posed by ageing.

This introductory chapter attempts to set out the main messages and conclusions in an integrated way that cuts across traditional disciplines. In the OECD jargon, this is the "horizontal" story about the policy implications of ageing societies. The following chapters address these issues in more depth following the more familiar structure – effects on policies for pensions, health and long-term care and labour markets. A concluding chapter deals with the overall consequences for fiscal policy and national savings.

B. Ageing populations and active ageing: a deepening of policy analysis

Populations in OECD countries are getting older. Today, many countries have "favourable" demographics, with the baby boomers of working age supporting relatively fewer retired people. However, by the second decade of the next century, the baby-boom generation will have reached retirement age, while the working-age population will fall in many OECD countries. At the same time, people are living longer and the numbers of the very elderly – those aged 80 years and over – are rising sharply.

The same general pattern holds in most OECD countries although, as shown in the annex, there are important differences in the existing age structure and in the rate at which populations age. For example, by 2030 current projections show the working-age population (defined as 15 to 64 years) in the OECD area could be $4\frac{1}{2}$ per cent smaller than at its peak level in 2010. However, in many countries the fall may be much more pronounced – as much as 24 per cent in Germany, 18 per cent in Italy, 17 per cent in Japan and 15 per cent in both the Netherlands and Spain.

In 1990, the ratio of older people to people of traditional working age was 19 per cent in the OECD area. By 2030, this would nearly double to 37 per cent. In Japan, which in 1980 had one of the lowest ratios in the OECD, the ratio is now rising and could reach $44\frac{1}{2}$ per cent in 2030, one of the highest projected ratios in the OECD. In Europe, the ratios start to increase in this decade, with particularly rapid growth after 2010. In the United States, the ratio starts to increase only after 2010.

The effects of ageing depend on the allocation of time to work, learning, leisure and the giving and receiving of care by people of different ages. For example, formal education is still concentrated among young people, work among people in their middle years and leisure and chronic illness among older people. Changes in the age structure of the population can therefore have large effects on education, on the labour market and on the provision of pensions and dependent care. However, patterns in the use of time are also evolving. For example, people are staying in school longer and retiring earlier in most countries. The participation of women in the labour market is growing, although considerable differences remain in participation rates across countries.

If policies are to encourage individuals, employers and social institutions to adjust quickly to changes in the economic situation or personal circumstances – with less need for government remedial action – they need to be sensitive to the combined effect of ageing and changing life-course arrangements. They should recognise, for example, the importance of learning and provisions for gradual transition to retirement among older workers *and* the growing numbers of older workers.

Much existing public policy does not take these life-cycle and ageing considerations into account. Traditional policies assume instead that people pass through three quite separate stages of life: education is almost exclusively for the young; pensions provide a separate secure stream of income security for older people; in the middle years, there are stable jobs and families and social security programmes are there for the exceptional times when these are missing.

Traditional policies therefore tend to have shortcomings that are increasingly evident: *a)* when the assumed stability in jobs or family is not there; *b)* for life stages which are not taken into account in the simple model, such as dependent care for frail elderly; *c)* at the main transition points in life – from school-to-work and work-to-retirement; and *d)* when actions at different stages of life re-enforce each other like traps related to low skills, low income and marginal jobs. It is in these areas where remedial action is most often required, and where reform agendas in many Member countries have been concentrated. Many of these reforms encourage a more integrated pattern of work, learning, leisure and care-giving over the entire life-course, including older ages. In this paper, such a more flexible allocation of time over the life-cycle is referred to as ''active ageing''.

What is important for policy is the combined effects of *individual ageing* (people living longer), *population ageing* (more people in older age groups as a consequence of the baby-boom and bust) and *active ageing* (changes in how time is spent in different age groups). The effects of individual ageing and population ageing have been the subject of considerable study for many years. These studies point to the challenges posed for public policy, but they are less helpful in pointing to solutions. Public policy can have little direct effect on population ageing; even enhanced migration, for example, could make only a small difference to the age structure of the population. However, the addition of an active ageing perspective holds promise of deepened policy analysis and increased policy effectiveness. There is much that government policies now do, and could do in the future, that influences the way in which people allocate activities over their lifetime.

Policy is often now supported by analysis that deals with shorter-term phenomena – the flexibility of the workforce in adjusting to current economic conditions, the responsiveness of investment decisions to capital markets, effectiveness in curing acute illness, or the training needed to meet specific skills needs. With an ageing and life-cycle perspective, policy analysis can also include a longer-term, more dynamic dimension by examining labour market and learning patterns, savings and investment decisions, health and illness, and equity and security – over people's *entire* lifetimes.

Analysis that takes account of these ageing and life-cycle considerations should lead to policies that are more coherent, without artificial distinctions between social and economic policy. It provides a helpful perspective on several long-standing policy problems. For example, issues related to equity look quite different, and perhaps more open to solution, when examined from a life-course perspective. Being out of work and receiving only a low income should not be seen as a problem *per se*, if that is a matter of choice – say to undertake full-time studies or to provide child or elder care. It is a problem if the flexibility is not there to enable people to return to the paid workforce, or if the opportunities to make such life-cycle choices are inequitably distributed.

With better life-cycle analysis, policies can be developed to give more appropriate recognition to the fact that what happens at one stage of life often has a large impact on other stages. There is increasing evidence, for example, that educational outcomes are driven by early childhood experiences in the home, that there are strong linkages between initial learning and learning (and productivity) later in life, that stress on the job is linked negatively to health and longevity, that work patterns do not match the patterns required for care of children and the dependent elderly, that physical and mental activity throughout life can slow down the loss of functions that are traditionally associated with ageing, and that income and health inequalities among adults are passed on to their children. There may also be differences among age cohorts that are relevant to policy, although the evidence here is less clear. (Age cohorts are people of similar ages who therefore have shared common historical experiences and have faced common economic conditions during their lives.)

Typical policy responses have included: the promotion of lifelong learning; the removal of arbitrary distinctions between the "old" and the "not-yet-old"; removing disincentives to flexible patterns of work that exist in some current programmes; promoting flexibility in working life arrangements; a stronger concentration on early childhood health and learning; the promotion of healthy life-styles; and more generally, a preference for preventive measures that affect people earlier in life rather than more costly remedial action later in life. The traditional focus on inequalities associated with earned income and the tax/transfer system becomes broadened to include matters like the intergenerational transmittal of wealth – and care – within the family, and the effects of family formation and break-up on family income.

The data and policy analysis to support such initiatives are still generally underdeveloped. As the analytic capacity develops, there is potential for incorporating ageing and life-course considerations in a much wider range of social and economic programming, including the measurement of effectiveness.

C. The effects of ageing

Effects on individuals and families

Ageing means that less time is being spent in paid work to support more time in other activities. Schooling and retirement are now lasting longer, and the proportion of time spent in traditional "working-age" years is shrinking correspondingly. During those "working" years, there are offsetting trends. Women work more continuously, but there is also high unemployment and some involuntary part-time work in most Member countries. Most important, the number of people of "retirement age" will grow sharply.

Many older individuals gradually become frail and experience poor health and social separation when they are over the age of 80. But most people in their 60s and early 70s share many of the same health and social characteristics as younger adults. In each older age group there is a wide spectrum – ranging from people with little impairment to those with severe disability. Differences among people in the same age group are usually greater than across different ages. As a result, treating people aged 25 to 64 as being in a "working age" category, and everyone over the age of 65 as being in a separate "elderly" category, is no longer helpful in examining health, social needs, skills and the ability to learn.

Population ageing has affected men and women differently. They have different patterns of labour force participation, of transition from work to retirement and of care-giving. In addition, women earn lower wages, they live longer, live alone longer, and can have longer periods of frailty and poverty near the end of their lives.

For both men and women, there is an increase in the lifetime hours spent outside a traditional family unit. There is new concern about family arrangements for the care of the growing number of frail elderly.

Effects on income and wealth

Because there are so many differences among older people, any statement that treats older people as a single group should be treated with caution. Nevertheless, it is generally true that, in many countries, their economic status has improved over the past two decades relative to workers. This has occurred in part because of improved pension benefits and increased coverage, particularly during the period when the public pension systems were becoming mature. It may also result from generally favourable tax treatment. On the other hand, poverty (by any definition) has not been eradicated among older people. It remains a real problem, especially for widowed, divorced and never-married women.

The wealth position of older people, on average, also surpasses that of other groups, for the most part because they have had a longer period of time in which to accumulate assets. The most important asset for most older people is their own home. Moreover, many benefited from the real appreciation of property values and reduction in the real costs of fixed-interest mortgages as a result of inflation in the 1970s and early 1980s. Other significant forms of wealth usually are highly concentrated among a very small proportion of older individuals.

This leads to questions about fairness between generations. It is today's younger people who will have to shoulder most of the burden of adjustment that results from the combination of demographics and the commitments embedded in existing pension arrangements. If the existing pension contract is to be honoured for existing retirees or near retirees, it is today's younger workers who will have to pay most of the costs, one way or the other. At least for the short- and medium-term, the most that public policy can do is to change the form in which the adjustment takes place and make small alterations in the way the burden falls on different generations. Some observers predict that this might result in rising inter-generational tension, although to date there is little evidence to support this view.

Effects on the labour market and economy

Once the baby-boom generation reaches retirement age, there will be fewer people of traditional working age and the average age of those working will rise. If all else remains the same, these changes might result in lower unemployment, shortages of young people in the workforce, and increased emphasis on lifelong learning, especially to cater to the training needs of older workers. However, OECD countries have already experienced some ageing of the workforce and yet rates of total and youth unemployment remain high. Other factors are clearly more important.

Current trends towards earlier retirement are likely to be moderated or reversed, as now appears to be happening in some Member countries. Some of this reversal will happen automatically in response to market forces and some will be the consequence of policy decisions to remove incentives towards early retirement embedded in social programmes.

There are also changes in the age structure of the workforce. Recently, the encouragement of earlier retirement and reduced hiring of the young has been a common corporate response to downsizing pressures. In many enterprises and governments the results are a concentration of people in their middle years. This changing age profile poses challenges for the management of human resources, including issues like reduced opportunity for upward mobility, pay policy, age discrimination, impacts on working-life flexibility, on child care and other family measures, on skills and productivity and, more generally, on the flexibility of organisations to adjust to changing markets.

Ageing populations have effects on the economy that go well beyond the labour market. Consumption patterns change and there are resulting changes in the structure of the economy and in the kinds of jobs available – as well in the skills of the workers who will fill those jobs. In some countries, but not all, there has been a major shift towards services aimed at people over 65, particularly in health and long-term care and in leisure and tourism. More work is needed to explore the consequences for the participation of older workers in the labour market and the effects on the voluntary sector.

Ageing also results in changed patterns of saving, investment and capital accumulation. Ageing populations tend to reduce national savings. Certainly this is the case for government savings, because of the spending pressures created. Private savings may also to be lower, but the evidence here is not as clear. The links between national savings, investment and living standards are also less clear, but give cause for concern. Current estimates suggest that, if policies are not changed, national savings might decline quite dramatically. In some countries net national savings might even be negative.

Effects on public policy

The design and administration of government programmes, especially health, education, social policies and active labour market programmes, will be affected by changes in the age characteristics of their participants. In cases such as lifelong learning and the care of frail older people, the appropriateness of existing policies, and the co-ordination of programmes and service delivery, may be called into question. Given the strains that ageing populations will place on public spending, it is more important than ever that programmes and policies be well designed to meet their objectives in the most efficient manner.

The largest pressure on public finance will be from public pensions. Potential increases in pension costs raise important issues about financing, benefit levels, eligibility, and incentive structures. In some countries, the effects of ageing on health care costs are likely to be significant; and, in all countries, there are likely to be increased costs associated with dependent care for the frail older people. While demographic changes should put less pressure on public spending on education and child benefits as the number of children declines, the effect is likely to be small in relation to the growth of pension costs.

Responding to the pervasive effects of ageing populations, and to greater flexibility in how time is spent over the life-cycle, may strain the present consultative processes and decision-making structures of government, at a time when building support among major constituencies will be essential. Developing coherent responses to these multi-dimensional effects requires a re-examination of the ways that governments gather data, evaluate policies, manage budgets, reconcile short- and long-term goals, co-ordinate activities among programme departments and central agencies and build consensus.

Looking further ahead

Analysis of the effects of ageing usually examines past trends in behaviour by age group. However, an approach based on extrapolating from the past may be unduly pessimistic. Older workers of 2010 will be better educated than those of today. Octogenarians of 2030 will be healthier than their parents or grandparents and women octogenarians will have worked longer. These factors are likely to have positive effects on health, employment and income security. They provide a basis for optimism about the eventual success of longer-term reforms.

D. Policy challenges and responses

Ageing populations and changes in life-course patterns, in conjunction with other factors, create four fundamental challenges for public policy.

The first is fiscal. If present policies are continued, ageing populations will result in large increases in government spending. At the same time, GDP growth is likely to slow unless productivity growth increases sharply, because growth in the working-age population will slow and even become negative in a number of countries. Increased productivity will mean that living standards, measured as GDP per person, will still rise, but at a much slower pace. In the absence of major policy reforms, public debt levels relative to GDP will rise dramatically in a number of countries.

The second challenge relates to market responsiveness – to establish a policy framework within which labour and capital markets are able to respond quickly and flexibly to changes in both the demand and supply of labour and capital that are likely to result from shifting demographics. The structural reforms that have been a focus of OECD discussions in recent years provide a cornerstone for such a policy framework. As people live longer and adapt to change, they will need to be able to move easily from one job to another and to receive clear market signals about the value of investment in education and training. They will also need to receive clear market signals that enable them to make trade-offs between consumption and saving and work and leisure.

The third challenge, encouraging active ageing, is focused on the effects of ageing on individuals – helping people to stay active, flexible and self-reliant as they age, with increased choice over the allocation of time throughout their life-course. Of particular concern is the growing numbers of people in the age groups where the transition from work to retirement occurs and among the very elderly where chronic health care problems are concentrated. In terms of policy solutions, research suggests that interventions earlier in life – in early childhood development, in high levels of generic skills in school, in active life-styles throughout life – are likely to be more effective than remedial interventions later in life and, more generally, that greater flexibility in allocating time over the life-course would have positive economic, social and health effects.

The fourth challenge relates to a new balance between collective and individual responsibilities. Reduced spending by government can be compensated for in part by a stronger private role, which in turn raises question of regulation and the roles of different actors in the private sector. While more flexible arrangements over the life-cycle, reduced government spending and a shift to greater private responsibility will give many people greater control over their lives and opportunity to succeed, for some it could simply mean more insecurity. People need to be confident that they will have adequate and equitable access to health and dependent care, to lifelong learning and other avenues that allow success in a more flexible world, to income security in retirement and, as a last resort, to a safety net. That confidence is now weak in some areas. For example, many younger people in Member countries have no confidence that public pensions will be there for them when they retire. In general, older people are in better economic circumstances than was once the case and have less need for collective support. However, this does not apply to all groups and a new balance of responsibilities must take into account the needs of people in different social and economic circumstances.

These are major, inter-related challenges. Moreover, unless reforms in response to these challenges are co-ordinated under a coherent strategy, there is a risk they may pull in different directions. An overall strategy may also be an important catalyst in building public support for reform, and in overcoming institutional difficulties.

Lack of public understanding is an important obstacle to building consensus and public support for change. Public debate in the area of pensions, for example, is often confused. And many important policy initiatives may lack strong public appeal, especially when addressed in isolation. Some do not have immediate payoffs. Some will have significant distributional consequences and may be sensitive to the growing number of potentially well-organised older voters. Building consensus on long-term solutions may not fit well with the political time horizon and the priorities of the next election. Part of the solution is to ensure that the broader ageing reform strategy incorporates various initiatives in a way that takes account of short- and long-term considerations and that is generally perceived to be reasonable and fair.

There are also institutional barriers to reform which derive, in part, from a fatalistic belief that ageing populations have inevitable fiscal effects and that there is little that governments can do in response other than general belt-tightening.[1] The analysis in this paper suggests that, to the contrary, much can be done through co-ordinated action on many fronts. However, taking concerted action is difficult. Many departments and government agencies must be involved – in service delivery, in policy formulation and in the role of government as a large employer. A comparable need for co-ordination exists with respect to organisations and professional disciplines outside government that must be active participants in achieving the changes needed. For example, reforms in the area of chronic care require close co-operation among professional disciplines – medicine, social work, finance and insurance – that traditionally have not worked closely together. A clear strategy is needed to clarify roles and responsibilities and to encourage coherent action.

Such reforms are summarised in Table 1.1 which assesses them against the four challenges: fiscal, market responsiveness, active ageing, and balancing individual and collective responsibility.

E.   Directions for reform

Pensions

Pension costs will increase and, one way or the other, the bulk of those costs must be borne by the younger generation – people now under the age of 40. The goal of reform is to find the most reasonable way of making the adjustment, to share the costs to the extent possible, and to put into place pension systems which are sustainable for future generations.

Gradually increasing the age of entitlement to retirement benefit, with actuarial adjustments for those who retire at different ages, is a central element in responding to the fiscal, market responsiveness and active ageing challenges. However, increasing the age of entitlement to full benefits, or increasing flexibility in pension arrangements during the work-to-retirement transition do not, by themselves, ensure that appropriate jobs will be there for older workers or that there will be an increase in the total number of lifetime hours worked. The extent to which raising the age of entitlement will also raise the *effective* age of retirement depends on the current age of entitlement (which varies from 60 to 67 in OECD countries) and on the existing gap between the effective age and the entitlement age. Pension reforms are a necessary supplement to, not a substitute for,

Table 1.1A. **Pensions, health and long-term care: possible directions for reform in light of the challenges posed by ageing populations**

Possible directions for reform	Potential for dealing with the challenges raised by ageing populations				Other observations
	Fiscal	Market responsiveness	Active ageing	Individual-collective balance	
Pensions					
Raising standard age of entitlement to benefit with actuarial adjustment for retirement at different ages • directly • indirectly by increasing contribution period for full benefit	Major gains in longer-term	Increase in labour supply	Extends active working life on a flexible basis	Increases individual choice in work-retirement transition	Success depends on the availability of appropriate jobs for older workers
Untargeted reductions in benefits • directly lowering the earnings-replacement rate or the level of flat-rate benefits • not fully indexing benefits • calculating earnings over a longer period	Major gains in longer-term depending on the degree of reduction	Little direct effect	Little direct effect	Encourages private pensions, mainly for those with higher incomes	Increases risk of poverty as benefits are reduced
Targeted reductions in benefits • directly or through taxation • reducing covered earnings ceilings • removing preferential income tax treatment	Major fiscal gains in longer-term, depending on degree of targeting and generosity of pensions	Little direct effect	Little direct effect	Encourages private pensions for those with higher incomes	Discourages private provision by those close to qualifying for public pensions
Increased contribution rates or shifts to other forms of taxation	Only modest gains realistic	Likely to discourage work and/or savings	Little direct effect	Little direct effect	

Table 1.1A. **Pensions, health and long-term care: possible directions for reform in light of the challenges posed by ageing populations** *(cont.)*

Possible directions for reform	Potential for dealing with the challenges raised by ageing populations					Other observations
	Fiscal	Market responsiveness	Active ageing	Individual-collective balance		
	Health and long-term care					
Research and development on the effectiveness of interventions and on chronic conditions such as Alzheimer's disease	Current investment needed, but with potentially significant longer-term gains	A healthier work-force	Reduced dependency	No direct effect		
Prevention of illness and promotion of health	Current investment needed, but with potentially significant longer-term gains	A healthier work	Reduced dependency	No direct effect		Evaluation of the outcomes of various interventions is important
Education and training of health personnel in geriatric care	Uncertain. Should mean more cost-effective medical practices	No direct effect	Reduced dependency	No direct effect		
Reforming long-term care • treating long-term care as a normal risk • ensuring that financing pools risks and covers the largest costs • balanced across disciplines • affordable in terms of both public and private expenditure	Helps control the extent of cost increases	No direct effect	Reduced dependency	Increased collective responsibility for costs		Dependent care can be seen as a separate stage in the life-cycle with its own requirements for public policy

Source: OECD.

Table 1.1B. Labour market, capital market, fiscal and other effects: possible directions for reform in light of the challenges posed by ageing populations

Possible directions for reform	Potential for dealing with the challenges raised by ageing populations				Other observations
	Fiscal	Labour market			
		Market responsiveness	Active ageing	Individual-collective balance	
Ensuring coherent policies, including mechanisms to co-ordinate reforms undertaken by employers and employee representatives as well as within governments.	Indirect effect, by reducing reliance on government expenditures	Indirect effect	Indirect effect	No direct effect	
Supporting smooth transitions from work to retirement • flexible working life arrangements • partial pensions • actuarial adjustments to pensions for early retirement • review of earnings rules and means tests in pensions	Long-term fiscal gains, but may be some short-term costs	Work force that is more flexible and potentially larger	Encourages active approach	Increases individual choice	Such measures are in place in a number of countries
Reforming public benefit entitlements. To remove disincentives to work in programming related to invalidity, unemployment insurance, etc. – and to remove incentives to abrupt early retirement	Significant fiscal gains may be possible	Removes distortions to market signals	Removes disincentives to active ageing	Encourages self-reliance	The goal is to make programming neutral over the longer-term with respect to life-cycle choices
Helping older workers maintain work-force attachment • life long learning, active labour market programming • review seniority provisions in pay scales • age discrimination and stereotyping	Uncertain	A more skilled, flexible work force	Encourages active approach	Increased individual choice	

Table 1.1B. **Labour market, capital market, fiscal and other effects: possible directions for reform in light of the challenges posed by ageing populations** *(cont.)*

Possible directions for reform	Potential for dealing with the challenges raised by ageing populations					Other observations
	Fiscal	Market responsiveness	Active ageing	Individual-collective balance		
Fiscal effects, capital markets and savings						
Improving fiscal positions, including cutting non-age related expenditure	Scope for significant fiscal gains	Higher national savings	No direct effect	Depends on specific option		Because of debt dynamics, the sooner cuts are made the larger the beneficial effect
Review of regulations with respect to private pensions funds and to health and long-term care insurance	No direct effect	Better operation of capital markets	No direct effect	A precondition for major increase in private role		
Other						
Policy effectiveness package, outlining the means by which governments can incorporate ageing considerations into their decision-making structures • statistics, evaluations • research funding priorities • decision-making and consultative structures • role of government as employer	Long-term fiscal gains, but may be some short-term costs	Provides clearer signals about government intentions	Important	No direct effect		
Public information that promotes life-cycle flexibility	Long-term fiscal gains, but may be some short-term costs	More flexible work force	Important	No direct effect		In some cases, may be best done outside government, possibly with public support

Source: OECD.

21

effective economic and social policies designed to raise employment and output and to increase working-life flexibility.

Increasing the effective age of retirement is not only an issue of affordability. It is also about the extent to which, in an uncertain world, the spending choices of coming generations will be pre-empted. Inaction on pension reform locks away an increasing share of GDP for decades to come. Coming generations may well have more important priorities than allocating ever-increasing shares of national income to support ever-increasing amounts of leisure at the end of life.

Increasing the average age of entitlement to benefits will be an important part of pension reform packages in most countries, but it is not a panacea. Chapter 2 describes other important pension issues that need to be addressed, including those, such as greater targeting of benefits, that may produce fiscal savings over a somewhat shorter time horizon than would be possible by raising the age of entitlement to benefits. The fiscal effects of various reform scenarios are examined.

Chapter 2 also describes more fundamental changes in the balance between individual and collective responsibilities for pensions, including the roles of pay-as-you-go and advanced funded elements, the roles of defined-benefits and defined-contributions, and of individual and company plans. While there is no ''best'' balance that can apply in all countries, public confidence in the pension contract would be strengthened by a clear statement of longer-term directions and by shorter-term reforms that were seen to moving towards longer-term goals.

Health and long-term care

Health and, especially, long-term care expenditures are heavily concentrated among older people, particularly among the very old. Chapter 3 examines the current state of knowledge about the effects of ageing on health and on health care expenditure in OECD countries. Several cost projections are presented although these are subject to much greater uncertainty than pension projections. Ageing presents a particularly difficult challenge for systems of long-term care, where new approaches are needed with respect to both service provision and financing.

In order to respond to ageing populations, there would be potentially large cost savings from shifting priorities in health research towards chronic conditions. Prevention and promotion become even more important, as does a refocussing in the education and training of health personnel. While there is no single best solution in the chronic care area, it has been possible to develop a set of common goals against which specific proposals can be assessed. A key goal is to treat long-term care as a normal life risk and to look to solutions that involve collective risk-pooling mechanisms. Another goal is to shift the focus of government policy towards dealing with major costs such as long-term nursing care; presently these are not covered as completely as some minor costs which individuals could more easily cover themselves. Affordability and an appropriate balance of service are other goals.

Labour market

Chapter 4 turns to a discussion of the effects of ageing on the labour market and areas for policy action. The challenge is to remove barriers to work, while maintaining or increasing productivity growth, and thereby to increase labour income. This will both reduce the costs associated with ageing populations and increase the resources that can be used to deal with ageing issues. In other words, the problem is the same as that addressed by the *OECD Jobs Study*. The chapter concentrates on the critical issues associated with employment among the growing numbers of older workers.

As noted, the fiscal, market responsiveness, and active ageing challenges all point to the desirability of increasing the effective age of retirement by extending work later in life, preferably on a gradual basis involving flexible part-time working arrangements. Such arrangements would allow retirement decisions to become much more responsive to individual preferences and changing economic circumstances.

Many countries have made progress in this direction, but a fixed age of retirement – and the use of early retirement as an adjustment mechanism in corporate restructuring – have become a widespread expectation in society and in the culture of enterprises. Solutions will have to involve close co-operation among governments, employers and employee representatives to address many inter-related issues. For example, if the disincentives to work are reduced in one social programme like pensions, the possibility arises that early retirement may still take place through other programmes such as invalidity or active labour market programmes, unless these are also reformed to prevent this from happening. Similarly, employers have little to gain in investing in the training of older workers if public programmes, in effect, subsidise the layoff of older workers in a period of down-sizing.

Some of the actions needed are under the control of public authorities: removing the incentives to retire early and abruptly that exist in public pensions and other social programmes; avoiding decisions that send the wrong signals such as using early retirement as a form of employment policy; introducing partial pension arrangements and actuarial adjustments to full pensions for people who retire at different ages; promoting active lifestyles that include part-time work; or designing age-specific active labour market programming. Employers and unions must play a lead in the removal of similar incentives to early retirement that exist in private pensions, in improving the portability of pensions, in promoting training and lifelong learning for older workers, and gradually changing a range of personnel practices that work against older workers. These include countering age discrimination in the work place, finding alternatives to pay scales that are based on seniority and hence drive up the cost of older workers, and developing flexible working-life arrangements, work organisation and working conditions designed to meet the needs of older workers.

Fiscal effects, national saving and capital markets

In the absence of reform, ageing populations will result in increasing government expenditure as a share of GDP. Projections of these fiscal effects are described in

Chapter 5. Higher expenditures could be offset by higher payroll contributions, but in most countries the required increases would be unacceptably high. It would also be possible to turn to other forms of taxation, but the chapter shows that there is little room to manœuvre here.

Ageing, by increasing current government spending, will reduce government saving and, although the evidence is less clear, may also decrease private savings. National savings are therefore likely to fall as a consequence of ageing populations, with significant impacts on the amount of investment undertaken.

A main part of the solution is to limit the increase in government expenditures and to take measures to do so early. Other elements include policies to support economic growth and employment along the lines discussed in the OECD in recent years, as well as the reforms described in this paper that are more directly linked to ageing and life-cycle flexibility.

Decreased government spending can be compensated for, in part, by increased private activity, particularly in the areas of private pensions, channelled through well-functioning capital markets. Therefore, ageing is likely to have important effects on the operation of capital markets. At the same time, well-functioning capital markets are a key factor in supporting some of the envisaged pension systems. In many countries, this is likely to result in a review of the regulatory framework, particularly with respect to pension funds. Pension assets in the OECD area now total more than $6 trillion, an amount that may double by the year 2000 and continue to grow thereafter. This raises issues of competition among private operators, disclosure and transparency, pension portability, external versus internal management, and rules that limit investment in equity or in foreign securities. For example, the share of foreign securities in these assets is small. Regulations will need to be reviewed if pension funds are to reap the diversification benefits that can be obtained by investing in the stock markets of the emerging economies.

Need for early action

Because the challenges are difficult, there is a temptation to postpone action – a temptation that must be resisted. It is hard to build consensus for changes in areas like increased age of entitlement to pension benefits at a time of high unemployment for older workers, even if the change takes effect a decade or more in the future when current labour market conditions will be irrelevant. It is also true that countries have been living with ageing populations for some time, apparently without disastrous consequences – living standards have not fallen along with the reduction in time spent at work. However, this has been a temporary respite. It has been mainly the result of increasing labour market participation among women which may not continue indefinitely, and increased social spending by government which cannot be relied on for the future.

Waiting for a more favourable economic time before taking action does not make sense. Postponing action is likely to lead to the need for even more drastic reforms later. Long lead times and advance warning are needed to allow people time to plan and adjust, especially to changes in pensions.

F.   Proposals for Phase 2 of the study

Ageing considerations will be taken into account throughout the OECD as a dimension of ongoing work. An example is work in the Public Management Service on ways of strengthening the capacity of governments to include long-run considerations in the policy process, an exercise which will address some of the institutional problems in developing coherent reform strategies.

With additional resources, two possible levels activity in a second phase are outlined: a *core level* of activity which would maintain progress on ageing themes without getting into any one area in depth; and an *expanded level of activity* that would cover selected areas in more depth and have greater involvement of countries and experts. The following proposals reflect discussion at the Employment, Labour and Social Affairs Committee (ELSAC) meeting in April 1996.

Core project

Over an 18-month period, a core project could provide practical examples to illustrate ways of implementing the policy directions discussed in this paper, it could extend the analysis of the effects of ageing, and it could begin to explore some of the new avenues suggested by the framework outlined in the document.

Best practices and lessons to be learned. This would be a practical review of the experience of countries in responding to the ageing challenges. It would not be a comprehensive survey, but rather would draw on existing analyses of initiatives in areas such as work-to-retirement transitions, pensions (including designs for greater targeting of pension benefits), lifelong learning, working-life arrangements, active labour market programmes, long-term care (including options for the financing and delivery of long-term care in both the public and private sectors), and social marketing that promotes active ageing concepts. The object would be a reference document that would help countries in the practical design of initiatives. It would identify common threads among successful interventions – whether in health, or labour market or learning.

Extending the analysis. Phase 1 was based on existing cross-country studies. The result is a review of the policy effects of ageing that is reasonably comprehensive but that is somewhat uneven in its coverage. By addressing this imbalance, it would be possible to produce a publication that could help build broader understanding of the nature of needed reforms. This would involve extending the analysis in areas such as the effects of ageing on the labour market and learning (in addition to the material on older workers that is covered in Chapter 4), human resource practices in enterprises (and in governments, where internal human resource practices could – but sometimes do not – set an example in areas such as early retirement), effects on social protection systems in addition to pensions, migration, the effects of ageing on the voluntary sector, and the broader social and health effects of active ageing. As well, a number of avenues were opened in Phase 1 – health care costs by age, cost projections based on alternative policies, equity and security from a life-cycle and inter-generational perspective – where some further cross-country analysis may result in useful insights on future directions for reform. Finally, there are a number of topics which deal with the economy-wide and international effects of ageing: reforms to pensions systems, including private sector provision; effects on corporate and private pension liabilities, which, like public pension plans, will come under pressure as the ratio of beneficiaries to payers rises (including regulatory and supervisory issues and the roles of different financial market institutions and capital markets); effects on private and national saving, investment and productivity as well as the inter-generational distribution of wealth and equity; and systemic issues, such as the effects on international capital flows both within the OECD and between the OECD and the non-OECD areas.

Exploring new directions. The work described above is mainly based on past studies and manipulations of existing data. The framework described in the paper suggests that there is considerable potential for exploring new avenues. For example, it would be useful to have better cross-country analysis on how ageing – and more flexible life-cycle patterns – affect voluntary activity and family care-giving, the flexibility and productivity of the labour force, private savings and inheritances, geographic mobility, patterns of consumption (and changes in the mix of skills that would result from changed demands for goods and services), housing and transport, and equity and social cohesion. It would be particularly helpful to have a greater understanding of the linkages that exist over life-courses among health, longevity, income, learning, care-giving and work. More specifically, a core project could have three products:

- A synthesis document that explores the policy implications that arise from the fragmentary cross-country data and research which now exist in these areas, that identifies key gaps in knowledge and areas of possible co-operation with organisations working in related areas. A longer-term work plan would fall out of this paper.
- A paper that reviews the availability of data on trends in the use of time over the life-cycle – the changing allocation of lifetime hours among work, leisure, learning, care giving and care-receiving. Sophisticated information is being developed in some countries – including longitudinal surveys, time use surveys, microdata and microsimulation models. In other countries, it will be important to understand the strengths and weakness of various proxy measures, such as analysis based on age cohorts and methods like recalculating existing labour force survey data to an hours basis. The document could identify future directions for data collection and analysis.
- Advice on the incorporation of ageing considerations into the decision-making and consultative processes in Member countries, including considerations related to social marketing, industrial relations, transparency and accountability, and techniques that allow identification of the life-course and inter-generational effects of programmes.

Expanded level of activity

With resources in addition to those needed in the core project, it would be possible to enrich the quality of the policy advice by gathering new data or embarking on new research, often in conjunction with other agencies. For example, the list of best practices and lessons to be learned could be updated to reflect current developments in countries, rather than relying solely on past reports. A number of Member countries at the ELSAC meeting pointed to the importance of several topics where further investigation would be needed. These included an exploration of the effects of ageing on the voluntary sector – and how this, in turn, affects market activities – effects on productivity, on production and consumption, on national saving and investment, and more emphasis on effects by gender and by socio-economic status. Generally, more investigation would be needed in order to give appropriate weight to the social as well as economic effects of ageing and life-cycle reform strategies.

The additional work would provide greater insight into the practical experiences of Member countries in response to the challenges of ageing, but it would not provide a comprehensive country-by-country follow-up on the effects of ageing, along the lines of the *OECD Jobs Study* follow-up. This would be premature and is **not** recommended for Phase 2.

An expanded second phase could also place more attention on consensus-building around policy directions, with greater emphasis on consultations with Member countries and experts. For example, there could be a conference or workshops with country experts to validate the usefulness of the ageing/active ageing framework – and the best practices – both to policy-makers and practitioners. Work could also proceed in resolving some apparent differences in the approach that different organisations have taken in considering the future public-private balance in the provision of retirement income. Finally, at the level of policy research and data development, co-operative work could begin with other national and international organisations that are studying the effects of ageing from a range of perspectives. (The core level of activity would be limited only to the identification of opportunities for such co-operation.)

Chapter 2

PENSIONS

A. Overview

Pension reform is being implemented or discussed in most Member countries. The debate usually centres around the long-term sustainability of public pensions. This reflects both a concern about the general fiscal situation and the more immediate effects of ageing populations on pensions – both public and private.

However, the debate also reflects a lack of public understanding about the nature of the pension contract, especially the nature of contributory public pensions. Although earnings-related contributory systems are usually pay-as-you-go arrangements like other taxes, they look like a form of savings and insurance to individuals, a perception supported by the way that pension contributions are often described as "credited" to individuals. People often wrongly believe that their contributions – and those of their employer – are for their own pensions, rather than a tax to support the pensions of the current generation of retirees. The result of this misunderstanding can be reduced public confidence in the pension system, and a lack of focus in public discussions, with consequent difficulties in gaining consensus around a reform package that deals with the real issues of fiscal sustainability.

The framework described in Chapter 1 can be used to clarify the debate over pension reform and to identify the problems that need to be given priority in those reforms.

First, with respect to the effects on *fiscal positions*, public pension expenditures have grown substantially from the time they were first implemented in OECD countries, and demographic shifts in the age composition of the population will aggravate these developments. As the "baby-boom" generation reaches retirement age in the early years of the next century in most countries, a working-age population of declining size will have to pay a much larger share of their earnings or income if current public benefit levels are maintained for future retirees.

Pension promises made in the past may have seemed affordable when made, but the effect of demographic changes was not always fully taken into account. Although the consequences of population ageing have been known for many years, due consideration was not always given to the affordability tomorrow of today's promises.

Second, with respect to meeting the *market responsiveness challenge*, pension policy can be one element of a larger strategy that increases the flexibility of the workforce and in the amount of time spent in work. Chapter 4 discusses other elements. Pension policy also has an impact on national savings, certainly with respect to government spending on pensions, but also on incentives for private savings. These issues are discussed at greater length in Chapter 5.

Third, with respect to effects on *active ageing*, actuarially-adjusted pensions are not always available for people who wish to retire at different ages. This, and other features of pensions, limit flexibility in the way that work and leisure are allocated in response to individual preferences and to the economic situation of the day. As well, maintaining a fixed age of entitlement to ''full'' retirement benefits means that, as longevity increases, there is a gradual but steady pressure towards spending more lifetime in retirement and fewer lifetime hours in work. Again, this reduces flexibility in the allocation of work, leisure, care and learning over lifetimes. Standard ages of entitlement to benefits are shown in Table 2.1.

Fourth, with respect to the need for a new balance between *individual and collective responsibilities*, there is a need to review the basic nature of the pension contract – to confirm or change the respective roles of pay-as-you-go or advanced funded elements, defined-benefits and defined-contributions, and public and private roles.

Demographic change means that the costs of pensions must rise. In all reform scenarios it is ultimately the younger generation, those who are currently less than 40 years of age, that must carry the burden of most of those costs. Compared with their parents' generation, they will have a *relatively* smaller net lifetime income relative to their own gross income from work – though not, if economic growth continues, *absolutely* smaller. The ways of shifting some of the burden to those who are retired or near retired are few. Depending on the nature of policy changes, the young will pay in foregone consumption by:

- paying higher taxes or contributions later, and suffering the economic consequences of increasing tax-to-GDP ratios;
- bearing the costs of higher public debt and, possibly, a reduction in the rate of national saving;
- facing lower income in retirement when gradual benefit reductions take effect;
- working longer and giving up leisure time;
- reducing current consumption to save more for their later years;
- or paying more now to improve the fiscal position when future obligations must be met.

In other words, there are no painless solutions. The younger generation will have to pay the bulk of the costs one way or another. The goal of reform is to find the most reasonable way of making the adjustment, to see whether the existing generation of older people can make at least some contribution to the cost, and to put systems of retirement income on a sustainable basis for coming generations.

Table 2.1. **Standard age of entitlement to public pension
in OECD countries, 1992**[1]

	Men	Women
United States	65	65
Japan	60	58
Germany	65	65
France[2]	60	60
Italy	60	55
United Kingdom	65	60
Canada	65	65
Australia	65	60
Austria	65	60
Belgium	65	60
Denmark	67	67
Finland	65	65
Greece	65	60
Ireland	66	66
Iceland	67	67
Luxembourg	65	65
Netherlands	65	65
Norway	67	67
New Zealand	61	61
Portugal	65	62
Spain	65	65
Sweden	65	65
Switzerland	65	62

1. Since 1992, the standard age has been increased in several countries. For example, in Japan the age for women is now 59. In Australia, it is 60.5. Other countries have announced gradual increases in the age of entitlement. For example, the standard age in the United States is scheduled to rise to 67.
2. For 37.5 years of social insurance contributions at a minimum.
Source: OECD (1995*a*).

B.   Responding to the fiscal challenge

Fiscal scenarios for pension expenditures

In order to help shed light on the magnitude of the fiscal problems and the impact that different broad types of pension reforms might have on government budgets, some illustrative scenarios have been constructed for most countries. Despite efforts to capture as fully as possible the institutional arrangements in each country, simplifying assumptions have been necessary, and the scenarios should be viewed as only broadly indicative. All scenarios assume that:

- all economies have returned to their medium-term growth path and there is no cyclical unemployment;

31

- medium term economic growth is determined by the projected growth of the working-age population and an assumed labour productivity growth rate of 1½ per cent per year;
- participation rates remain constant.[2] In scenarios where the age of entitlement to benefits rise, people who formerly would have been eligible for pensions are assumed to have the average participation rate across all workers of the same sex.

The *baseline scenario*, shown in Chart 2.1, illustrates the path of public pensions expenditures and contributions on the assumption that present pension rules (adjusted for announced reforms) are maintained. In this scenario, almost all countries face sharp increases in pension expenditures. But in some countries, pension expenditures will rise to much higher levels than others. For example, in Japan, Germany and Italy, pension expenditures would rise to more than 15 per cent of GDP, while in the United States, the United Kingdom and Canada, they remain at less than 10 per cent of GDP.

The alternative scenarios have been constructed purely for illustrative purposes and are designed to indicate a way of adapting the baseline scenario to reflect some of the issues that are being discussed in some Member countries. The relative costs between different scenarios depend crucially on the parameters chosen in each alternative scenario (such as 70 years for retirement ages, or capping expenditure from 2015 onwards). The parameters used may, in some countries, appear as extreme if viewed in light of the actual reform proposals. They are chosen simply to illustrate the scale of pension reform that would be needed to get significant fiscal results.

The baseline and alternative scenarios are summarised in net present value form in Table 2.2 and as annual contributions and expenditure flows in Table 2.3. The variations from the baseline scenario are shown in Chart 2.2.

The *later retirement scenario* gradually raises the age of entitlement to benefits to 70 years of age and assumes every year before that age is spent working and paying contributions. Under this scenario, upward pressure on pensions expenditures as a result of demographic pressures can be largely offset in most countries.

The *cost-containment scenario* limits total pension expenditure growth to the rate of growth of GDP from 2015 onwards, and budgetary pressures are reduced dramatically. It would correspond to practical reforms that made across-the-board cuts in benefit levels and indexation formulae. In many countries this would result in fiscal effects of about the same order as that in the later retirement scenario. However, it may be less realistic as a sustainable policy. Under this scenario, the value of the public pension received by each person (relative to average earnings) also would drop significantly – from just over 40 per cent of average wages in 2015 to around 30 per cent by 2030, on average in the major seven countries. The result of such a reform might be many more elderly living in relative poverty in the future, unless they accumulate additional savings to make up the shortfall.

A *targeting scenario* assumes that from 2010 onwards, replacement rates (benefits relative to wages) are held constant but the proportion of the elderly population that would get a pension gradually falls to 30 per cent. In other words, this scenario would correspond to proposals that would limit public pensions to those with lower incomes, and have middle and higher income groups relying on the private sector. The result, of

Chart 2.1. **Public pension payments and contributions**

As a percentage of GDP

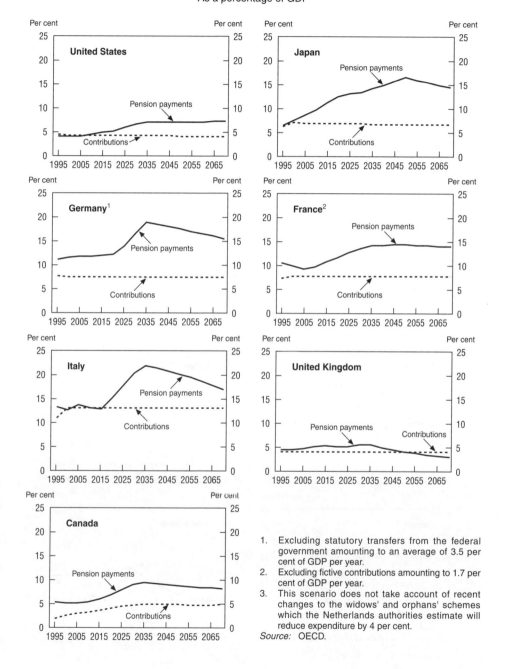

1. Excluding statutory transfers from the federal government amounting to an average of 3.5 per cent of GDP per year.
2. Excluding fictive contributions amounting to 1.7 per cent of GDP per year.
3. This scenario does not take account of recent changes to the widows' and orphans' schemes which the Netherlands authorities estimate will reduce expenditure by 4 per cent.

Source: OECD.

Chart 2.1. *(cont.)* **Public pension payments and contributions**
As a percentage of GDP

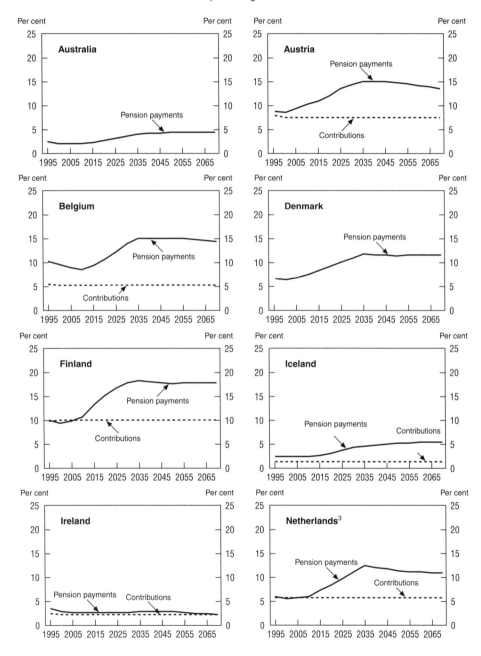

Chart 2.1. *(cont.)* **Public pension payments and contributions**
As a percentage of GDP

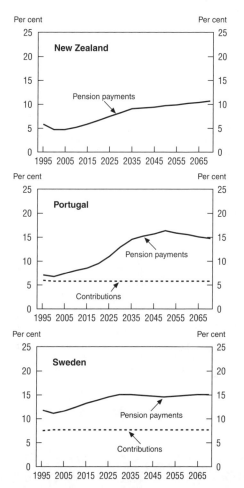

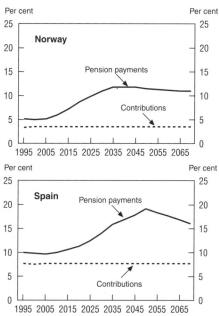

Table 2.2. **Net present value of pension contributions, expenditure and balances**[1]

As a percentage of 1994 GDP

		Baseline scenario	Cost containment scenario[2]	Wage indexation scenario[3]	Later retirement scenario[4]	Targeting scenario[5]
United States	Contributions	133.9	133.9	133.9	138.2	133.9
	Expenditure	162.5	142.1	177.4	141.7	108.0
	Balance[6]	–23.0	–2.6	–37.9	2.2	31.5
Japan	Contributions	192.2	192.2	192.2	200.7	192.2
	Expenditure	299.4	269.0	299.4	263.1	201.8
	Balance[6]	–70.0	–39.6	–70.0	–25.3	27.5
Germany	Contributions	286.3	286.3	286.3	301.1	286.3
	Expenditure	347.9	313.2	347.9	308.7	274.6
	Balance	–61.6	–26.9	–61.6	–7.6	11.7
France	Contributions	215.7	215.7	215.7	237.9	215.7
	Expenditure	317.8	289.3	351.8	253.0	228.2
	Balance	–102.1	–73.6	–136.1	–15.0	–12.5
Italy	Contributions	341.5	341.5	341.5	377.2	341.5
	Expenditure	401.3	347.7	451.9	347.4	315.4
	Balance	–59.7	–6.2	–110.3	29.8	26.1
United Kingdom	Contributions	118.2	118.2	118.2	124.1	118.2
	Expenditure	142.0	147.1	180.8	121.5	109.5
	Balance	–23.8	–28.9	–62.6	2.6	8.7
Canada	Contributions	97.4	97.4	97.4	103.4	97.4
	Expenditure	203.8	174.2	219.2	166.2	143.2
	Balance[6]	–100.7	–71.1	–116.1	–57.1	–40.1
Australia	Contributions	n.a.	n.a.	n.a.	n.a.	n.a.
	Expenditure	96.7	78.3	105.3	79.4	69.9
	Balance	–96.7	–78.3	–105.3	–79.4	–69.9
Austria	Contributions	205.4	205.4	205.4	218.5	205.4
	Expenditure	298.0	267.9	298.0	246.3	222.7
	Balance	–92.5	–62.4	–92.5	–27.8	–17.3
Belgium	Contributions	147.2	147.2	147.2	155.0	147.2
	Expenditure	299.8	259.9	323.6	251.5	212.6
	Balance	–152.6	–112.6	–176.4	–96.5	–65.3
Denmark	Contributions	n.a.	n.a.	n.a.	n.a.	n.a.
	Expenditure	234.5	210.6	234.5	179.4	149.8
	Balance	–234.5	–210.6	–234.5	–179.4	–149.8
Finland	Contributions	294.4	294.4	294.4	310.4	294.4
	Expenditure	384.2	340.9	408.4	303.9	266.9
	Balance[6]	–64.8	–21.6	–89.0	31.5	52.5
Iceland	Contributions	40.1	40.1	40.1	41.3	40.1
	Expenditure	106.3	82.6	106.3	91.3	88.3
	Balance	–66.2	–42.5	–66.2	–50.0	–48.2

Table 2.2. **Net present value of pension contributions,**
expenditure and balances[1] *(cont.)*

As a percentage of 1994 GDP

		Baseline scenario	Cost containment scenario[2]	Wage indexation scenario[3]	Later retirement scenario[4]	Targeting scenario[5]
Ireland	Contributions	89.2	89.2	89.2	93.4	89.2
	Expenditure	107.0	105.7	145.0	89.5	85.5
	Balance	−17.8	−16.5	−55.8	4.0	3.7
Netherlands[7]	Contributions	160.1	160.1	160.1	168.8	160.1
	Expenditure	213.5	180.5	234.3	178.6	145.1
	Balance	−53.3	−20.4	−74.2	−9.8	15.1
New Zealand	Contributions	n.a.	n.a.	n.a.	n.a.	n.a.
	Expenditure	212.8	177.6	212.8	171.4	136.1
	Balance	−212.8	−177.6	−212.8	−171.4	−136.1
Norway	Contributions	105.4	105.4	105.4	108.7	105.4
	Expenditure	229.5	189.4	251.4	200.7	146.0
	Balance	−124.1	−84.1	−146.0	−92.0	−40.7
Portugal	Contributions	167.7	167.7	167.7	175.9	167.7
	Expenditure	277.0	228.0	297.9	236.3	169.4
	Balance	−109.2	−60.2	−130.2	−60.4	−1.7
Spain	Contributions	214.7	214.7	214.7	226.2	214.7
	Expenditure	323.3	283.1	340.2	298.4	264.8
	Balance	−108.6	−68.3	−125.4	−72.2	−50.1
Sweden	Contributions	219.4	219.4	219.4	231.0	219.4
	Expenditure	369.6	354.3	391.4	257.8	322.6
	Balance[6]	−132.3	−117.0	−154.1	−8.8	−85.2

1. The net present value refers to today's value of future receipts and payments. The calculation assumes a discount rate of 5 per cent per year over the period 1994-2070.
2. Pension expenditures are frozen as a percentage of GDP from 2015.
3. Pension expenditures grow with wages from 2005.
4. Starting after 2005, retirement age is raised by 0.5 each year to reach 70 years of age.
5. Eligibility rates (ratio of pensioners to the retirement age population) are gradually decreased to 30 per cent over the period 2015-2030, while the replacement rate (average pensions to average wages) is frozen at its 2010 level.
6. Including pre-existing assets which amount to 5.8 per cent of GDP for the United States, 37.1 per cent of GDP for Japan, 5.7 per cent of GDP for Canada, 25 per cent of GDP for Finland and 18 per cent of GDP for Sweden.
7. These scenarios do not take account of recent changes to the widows' and orphans' schemes which the Netherlands authorities estimate will reduce expenditure by 4 per cent.

Source: OECD.

Table 2.3. **Pension expenditures under various scenarios**[1]

As a percentage of GDP in 1994 prices

		1995	2000	2010	2020	2030	2040	2050	2060	2070
United States	Baseline	4.1	4.2	4.5	5.2	6.6	7.1	7.0	7.2	7.4
	Cost containment	4.1	4.2	4.5	4.9	4.9	4.9	4.9	4.9	4.9
	Wage indexation	4.1	4.2	5.0	5.8	7.5	8.0	8.0	8.2	8.4
	Later retirement	4.1	4.2	3.6	3.9	5.1	5.7	5.7	5.9	6.1
	Targeting	4.1	4.2	4.5	3.4	2.0	2.1	2.1	2.2	2.3
Japan	Baseline	6.6	7.5	9.6	12.4	13.4	14.9	16.5	15.5	14.4
	Cost containment	6.6	7.5	9.6	11.2	11.2	11.2	11.2	11.2	11.2
	Wage indexation	6.6	7.5	9.6	12.4	13.4	14.9	16.5	15.5	14.4
	Later retirement	6.6	7.5	9.3	9.4	9.3	10.1	11.8	11.0	10.3
	Targeting	6.6	7.5	9.6	7.9	4.0	4.4	4.9	4.6	4.3
Germany	Baseline	11.1	11.5	11.8	12.3	16.5	18.4	17.5	16.5	15.5
	Cost containment	11.1	11.5	11.8	12.0	12.0	12.0	12.0	12.0	12.0
	Wage indexation	11.1	11.5	11.8	12.3	16.5	18.4	17.5	16.5	15.5
	Later retirement	11.1	11.5	10.7	9.0	10.6	12.6	12.8	12.3	11.7
	Targeting	11.1	11.5	11.8	8.8	7.8	8.8	8.3	7.8	7.3
France	Baseline	10.6	9.8	9.7	11.6	13.5	14.3	14.4	14.2	14.0
	Cost containment	10.6	9.8	9.7	10.7	10.7	10.7	10.7	10.7	10.7
	Wage indexation	10.6	9.8	10.8	13.5	15.8	16.8	17.0	16.8	16.5
	Later retirement	10.6	9.8	7.9	6.6	6.5	7.2	7.6	7.6	7.6
	Targeting	10.6	9.8	9.7	7.8	4.3	4.6	4.6	4.6	4.5
Italy	Baseline	13.3	12.6	13.2	15.3	20.3	21.4	20.3	18.7	17.0
	Cost containment	13.3	12.6	13.2	13.0	13.0	13.0	13.0	13.0	13.0
	Wage indexation	13.3	12.6	14.8	18.1	24.6	26.3	25.2	23.0	20.8
	Later retirement	13.3	12.6	12.8	11.7	10.5	8.8	10.2	9.3	8.3
	Targeting	13.3	12.6	13.2	11.5	8.9	9.5	9.2	8.3	7.5
United Kingdom	Baseline	4.5	4.5	5.2	5.1	5.5	5.0	4.1	3.6	3.1
	Cost containment	4.5	4.5	5.2	5.3	5.3	5.3	5.3	5.3	5.3
	Wage indexation	4.5	4.5	5.9	6.2	7.8	8.5	8.3	8.4	8.4
	Later retirement	4.5	4.5	4.3	3.7	3.4	3.3	2.9	2.5	2.2
	Targeting	4.5	4.5	5.2	3.2	1.9	2.0	2.0	2.0	2.0
Canada	Baseline	5.2	5.0	5.3	6.9	9.0	9.1	8.7	8.4	8.1
	Cost containment	5.2	5.0	5.3	6.0	6.0	6.0	6.0	6.0	6.0
	Wage indexation	5.2	5.0	5.2	7.2	10.0	10.8	10.9	11.0	11.1
	Later retirement	5.2	5.0	4.3	4.2	5.7	6.3	6.1	5.9	5.8
	Targeting	5.2	5.0	5.3	4.7	3.4	3.4	3.3	3.1	3.0
Australia	Baseline	2.6	2.3	2.3	2.9	3.8	4.3	4.5	4.6	4.6
	Cost containment	2.6	2.3	2.3	2.5	2.5	2.5	2.5	2.5	2.5
	Wage indexation	2.6	2.3	2.5	3.2	4.2	4.8	5.1	5.2	5.3
	Later retirement	2.6	2.3	1.9	1.8	2.4	2.9	3.2	3.2	3.3
	Targeting	2.6	2.3	2.3	2.1	1.7	1.9	2.0	2.1	2.1
Austria	Baseline	8.8	8.6	10.2	12.1	14.4	15.0	14.9	14.2	13.5
	Cost containment	8.8	8.6	10.2	10.9	10.9	10.9	10.9	10.9	10.9
	Wage indexation	8.8	8.6	10.2	12.1	14.4	15.0	14.9	14.2	13.5
	Later retirement	8.8	8.6	8.5	7.3	8.0	9.9	10.6	10.2	9.7
	Targeting	8.8	8.6	10.2	8.6	6.0	6.2	6.1	5.8	5.5

Table 2.3. **Pension expenditures under various scenarios**[1] *(cont.)*

As a percentage of GDP in 1994 prices

		1995	2000	2010	2020	2030	2040	2050	2060	2070
Belgium	Baseline	10.4	9.7	8.7	10.7	13.9	15.0	15.1	14.7	14.3
	Cost containment	10.4	9.7	8.7	9.5	9.5	9.5	9.5	9.5	9.5
	Wage indexation	10.4	9.7	9.5	11.9	15.6	17.0	17.1	16.7	16.3
	Later retirement	10.4	9.7	7.2	6.7	8.7	10.1	10.6	10.4	10.2
	Targeting	10.4	9.7	8.7	7.0	4.1	4.5	4.5	4.4	4.3
Denmark	Baseline	6.8	6.4	7.6	9.3	10.9	11.6	11.5	11.6	11.7
	Cost containment	6.8	6.4	7.6	8.5	8.5	8.5	8.5	8.5	8.5
	Wage indexation	6.8	6.4	7.6	9.3	10.9	11.6	11.5	11.6	11.7
	Later retirement	6.8	6.4	4.3	5.6	6.5	7.5	8.0	8.1	8.1
	Targeting	6.8	6.4	7.6	4.8	2.6	2.9	2.9	3.0	3.0
Finland	Baseline	10.1	9.5	10.7	15.2	17.8	18.0	17.7	17.7	17.8
	Cost containment	10.1	9.5	10.7	13.3	13.3	13.3	13.3	13.3	13.3
	Wage indexation	10.1	9.5	11.6	16.3	19.3	19.5	19.1	19.2	19.3
	Later retirement	10.1	9.5	8.1	8.8	11.2	11.8	11.6	11.8	12.0
	Targeting	10.1	9.5	10.7	10.1	6.1	6.2	6.1	6.1	6.1
Iceland	Baseline	2.5	2.4	2.4	3.1	4.2	4.8	5.2	5.4	5.5
	Cost containment	2.5	2.4	2.4	2.7	2.7	2.7	2.7	2.7	2.7
	Wage indexation	2.5	2.4	2.4	3.1	4.2	4.8	5.2	5.4	5.5
	Later retirement	2.5	2.4	1.9	2.3	3.2	3.8	4.1	4.3	4.4
	Targeting	2.5	2.4	2.4	2.6	2.9	3.3	3.6	3.7	3.8
Ireland	Baseline	3.6	2.9	2.6	2.7	2.8	2.9	3.0	2.6	2.2
	Cost containment	3.6	2.9	2.6	2.7	2.7	2.7	2.7	2.7	2.7
	Wage indexation	3.6	2.9	3.0	3.7	4.2	5.2	6.2	6.2	6.3
	Later retirement	3.6	2.9	2.1	1.8	1.8	1.9	2.0	1.8	1.6
	Targeting	3.6	2.9	2.6	2.0	1.1	1.4	1.7	1.7	1.7
Netherlands[2]	Baseline	6.0	5.7	6.1	8.4	11.2	12.1	11.4	11.2	11.0
	Cost containment	6.0	5.7	6.1	7.4	7.4	7.4	7.4	7.4	7.4
	Wage indexation	6.0	5.7	6.8	9.5	12.8	13.9	13.1	12.9	12.6
	Later retirement	6.0	5.7	5.1	5.5	7.2	8.3	8.6	8.4	8.2
	Targeting	6.0	5.7	6.1	5.5	3.4	3.7	3.5	3.4	3.4
New Zealand	Baseline	5.9	4.8	5.2	6.7	8.3	9.4	9.8	10.3	10.7
	Cost containment	5.9	4.8	5.2	6.0	6.0	6.0	6.0	6.0	6.0
	Wage indexation	5.9	4.8	5.2	6.7	8.3	9.4	9.8	10.3	10.7
	Later retirement	5.9	4.8	4.2	4.2	5.3	6.2	6.9	7.2	7.6
	Targeting	5.9	4.8	5.2	4.3	2.4	2.7	2.8	2.9	3.1
Norway	Baseline	5.2	4.9	6.0	8.6	10.9	11.8	11.5	11.1	11.1
	Cost containment	5.2	4.9	6.0	7.3	7.3	7.3	7.3	7.3	7.3
	Wage indexation	5.2	4.9	6.7	9.7	12.2	13.3	12.9	12.5	12.5
	Later retirement	5.2	4.9	4.9	6.6	8.5	9.4	9.5	9.2	9.1
	Targeting	5.2	4.9	6.0	5.4	3.1	3.5	3.5	3.5	3.6
Portugal	Baseline	7.1	6.9	8.1	9.6	13.0	15.2	16.5	15.6	14.8
	Cost containment	7.1	6.9	8.1	8.6	8.6	8.6	8.6	8.6	8.6
	Wage indexation	7.1	6.9	8.8	10.5	14.3	16.9	18.3	17.3	16.4
	Later retirement	7.1	6.9	6.8	6.4	8.5	11.2	12.8	11.8	11.1
	Targeting	7.1	6.9	8.1	5.6	2.3	2.9	3.3	3.2	3.0

Table 2.3. **Pension expenditures under various scenarios**[1] *(cont.)*

As a percentage of GDP in 1994 prices

		1995	2000	2010	2020	2030	2040	2050	2060	2070
Spain	Baseline	10.0	9.8	10.0	11.3	14.1	16.8	19.1	17.6	16.0
	Cost containment	10.0	9.8	10.0	10.6	10.6	10.6	10.6	10.6	10.6
	Wage indexation	10.0	9.8	10.6	12.1	15.2	18.3	21.0	19.2	17.5
	Later retirement	10.0	9.8	9.1	9.1	10.6	12.8	15.2	14.1	13.0
	Targeting	10.0	9.8	10.0	9.1	8.1	9.3	10.3	9.6	8.9
Sweden	Baseline	11.8	11.1	12.4	13.9	15.0	14.9	14.5	14.8	15.1
	Cost containment	11.8	11.1	12.4	13.3	13.3	13.3	13.3	13.3	13.3
	Wage indexation	11.8	11.1	13.2	15.1	16.4	16.3	15.9	16.3	16.6
	Later retirement	11.8	11.1	6.3	6.4	7.1	7.4	7.5	7.7	7.9
	Targeting	11.8	11.1	12.4	10.4	11.4	11.7	11.2	11.6	12.0

1. For definitions of the various scenarios, see the footnotes on Table 2.2.
2. These scenarios do not take account of recent changes to the widows' and orphans' schemes which the Netherlands authorities estimate will reduce expenditure by 4 per cent.
Source: OECD.

course, is a large change in public expenditures. This option differs from the cost-containment scenario under which everyone would get a pension, but a very small one. It addresses concerns about income disparities among the retired population, particularly those which result from lack of entitlement for an earnings-related pension.

The *wage-indexation scenario* illustrates reforms that move in the opposite fiscal direction and that would improve pension benefits. It assumes that all pensions are wage-indexed. Under existing public pension rules in almost all OECD countries, benefits are adjusted only for price increases during retirement. Under an earnings-related price-indexed regime, the relative living standards of pensioners decline as they grow older. Under the alternative of wage-indexing, the cost pressures would be exacerbated, by around 2 to 3 percentage points of GDP on average.

Incremental reform

As noted, the scenarios are only intended to illustrate the general order of effects, and should not be viewed as reform proposals in their own right. There is no ''best'' way to make pension reforms that will be appropriate in every country. What is ''best'' is linked to the starting position of a country – what it can afford and what promises were made earlier. Countries, in practice, are likely to consider a package of balanced reforms – some large and some small – throughout the entire system of retirement income: flat rate pensions, earnings-related pensions and the regulation and taxation of private pensions.

Chart 2.2. **Pension scenarios: variations from baseline**

Pension balances as a percentage of GDP

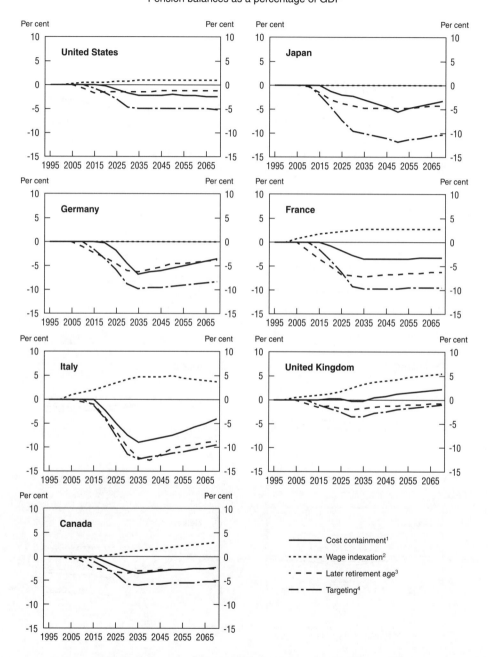

Cost containment[1]

Wage indexation[2]

Later retirement age[3]

Targeting[4]

Chart 2.2. *(cont.)*   **Pension scenarios: variations from baseline**
Pension balances as a percentage of GDP

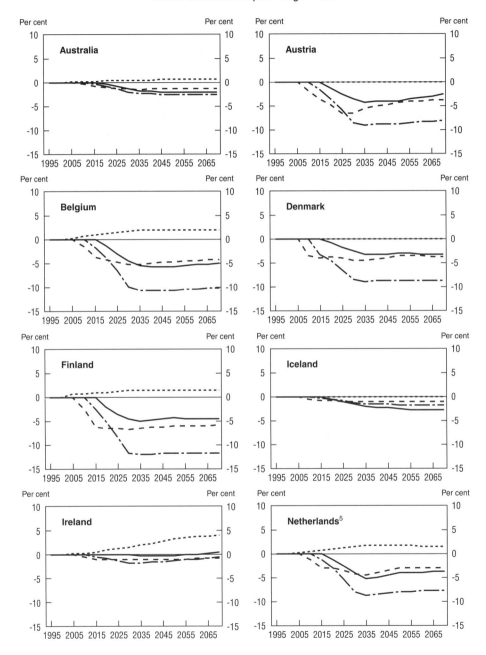

Chart 2.2. *(cont.)* **Pension scenarios: variations from baseline**
Pension balances as a percentage of GDP

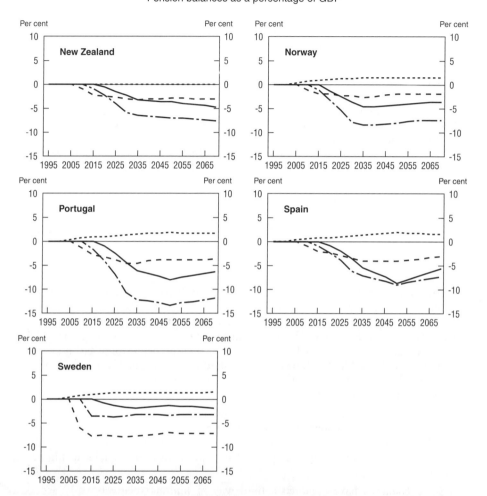

1. Pension expenditures are frozen as a percentage of GDP from 2015.
2. Pension expenditures grow with wages from 2005.
3. Starting after 2005, retirement age is raised by 0.5 each year to reach 70 years of age.
4. Eligibility rates (ratio of pensioner to the retirement age population) are gradually decreased to 30 per cent over the period 2015-2030, while the replacement rate (average pensions to average wages) is frozen at its 2010 level.
5. These scenarios do not take account of recent changes to the widows' and orphans' schemes which the Netherlands authorities estimate will reduce expenditure by 4 per cent.
Source: OECD.

Most OECD countries have mature pension schemes, and it may not be realistic to try to make changes that assume the slate is clean. The following section, therefore, outlines some directions for incremental reform that correspond to the goals associated with each of the three scenarios above that resulted in improved fiscal positions: later retirement, general cost containment, and targeted reforms.

Moving towards later retirement

Raising the age of entitlement to retirement benefits is a promising option, particularly in those countries that have a relatively low "standard" age of eligibility and where the gap between the existing effective age and the "standard" age of entitlement is not large. The total value of benefits would be lower, but monthly benefit amounts would not have to be reduced. Increased years of life mean that the years in retirement, on average, might not change.

Raising the age of entitlement reduces expenditure on pensions. If it also brings about an increase in the effective retirement age, it will also increase labour supply. While this will not lead to higher contributions relative to GDP, it should lead to higher levels of GDP and overall living standards. Where the gap between effective and standard entitlement ages is now large, other measures will likely be necessary to increase labour supply.

There are several ways of raising the age of entitlement. The most obvious way, and often the most difficult, is simply to postpone access to full benefits to a later age, coupled with actuarial reductions in benefits permissible at an earlier age. The major part of any savings to the system occurs after many years as the share of the beneficiary population that has been affected grows. This approach is being followed in Germany, Italy, Japan, the United States. Raising the standard retirement age for women to that for men (where they differ) has a similar effect and has been announced in Australia, New Zealand and the United Kingdom.

For contributory schemes, a second option which has a similar effect is to require longer years of work and contributions before a person is entitled to full benefits, with actuarial reductions for each year for which the pension has been anticipated. Savings to the system also occur mainly in later years. This reform has been implemented in France and Sweden.

Some countries have explored a third way of limiting relatively early access to pension benefits – by changes involving the required vesting period – for example, the number of years a person must contribute to the scheme, or must be a resident of the country in order to qualify for any public pension at all. A relatively short vesting period results in extensive coverage, but with correspondingly higher pension expenditures. A relatively long vesting period results in larger numbers of people who do not receive contributory pension benefits at retirement, despite being obliged to pay contributions. Because of this element of income redistribution, extending the vesting period is not an attractive way of pursuing savings.

Countries will need to be sensitive, in raising standard ages of entitlement, to the particular concerns of different categories of workers and different working conditions, including those who have spent their lives in hard physical labour and people with disabilities.

Moving towards general cost containment

Across-the-board cuts to pensions in payment could be made directly by cutting replacement rates in earnings-related schemes or reducing the amount of flat-rate benefits. Alternatively, such cuts could be made indirectly by changing the approach used for indexation.

In an earnings-related scheme with a defined-benefit formula (discussed below), a reduction of the replacement rate is effectively a reduction in the accrual factor, that is, in the value of each year of employment and of contributions. Significant expenditure savings would occur if it were implemented for all new retirees. The effect of such a change on labour supply is less clear. While generous benefit levels make retirement at the earliest opportunity more feasible, reducing the value of working longer because of lower pension accruals affects work incentives in the opposite direction. It is unclear *a priori* which effect will be stronger.

In some countries, there also is a minimum benefit award in social insurance pension structures. In a flat-rate scheme, a reduction in this minimum would only reduce costs to the extent that costs to means-tested programmes did not increase.

Indexing pension payments to movements in average wages permits pensioners to share in the fruits of economic growth. As long as average wage growth exceeds growth in other prices, as is usually the case, wage-indexing is also more costly. The less costly alternative of indexing to changes in consumer prices maintains the purchasing power of benefits at the time they were first received, but it also results in declines in the relative economic status of pensioners over time, as long as real wages continue to rise. Therefore, many countries already have moved away from full wage-indexing of benefits, and adjust benefits automatically to some proportion of average wage movements or to consumer prices.

A reduction in the indexing factor is one of the few changes that can have a substantial current-period impact on the budget. A temporary reduction, as well as a permanent one, also will have a cumulative impact over time since the base amounts which are indexed are *permanently* reduced in either case. Obviously, a permanent change will result in a larger reduction and larger budgetary savings over the long-term. But it also would have a particularly significant effect on flat-rate benefits, and would erode their value over time to a much greater extent than in the case of wage-related benefits.

The various formulae used to calculate pension benefits could be changed. In defined-benefit schemes, one avenue would be to make changes in the calculation of average earnings. Benefits are determined by averaging earnings over some period. The longer the period, the lower the average is likely to be, since both high and low (or zero) earnings will be included. Formulae which use a relatively short period immediately prior to retirement are biased toward those whose earnings increase over the life-cycle and are therefore potentially inequitable as well as being costly. Lengthening the averaging

45

period reduces the base on which benefits are calculated and can, therefore, reduce benefits and costs. This approach has been followed, for example, in the United States and many other countries.

In general, untargeted, across-the-board cuts are not a major avenue for short- and medium-term fiscal savings. Many changes to the pension "contract" have significant effects only in the longer-term because they need to be phased-in gradually. People need to know how much they will receive some years in advance in order to make adequate preparation for their retirement. Once retired, they have little or no flexibility to adjust to retroactive changes. But even when implemented immediately, the major effects of some changes occur much later because relatively few beneficiaries are affected in early years.

Moving towards greater targeting

Another option for fiscal savings is to reduce costs in a more targeted fashions, reducing the pension benefits for higher income earners somewhat more than for low-income earners. Apart from the direct application of means testing to pensions, there are several other ways of achieving this. In earnings-related schemes, the covered earnings ceiling could be reduced, either in nominal terms or by eliminating the indexation of the earnings ceiling. Table 5.4 shows current ceilings.

As discussed further in Chapter 5, the same earnings ceiling often applies to contributions. If contributions and benefits are simultaneously reduced, no fiscal gain would occur. For this change to result in fiscal savings, it would be necessary to break the link between the benefit and contribution base, by maintaining contributions up to a higher ceiling. However, such a change would violate the relation between pension contributions and entitlements. It is possible to mask the problem by reducing the contribution ceiling for employees and maintaining it its former level, or raising it, for employers. This charge on employers will eventually have an impact on pre-tax wages; if it does not, the higher labour costs to employers will depress employment.

Increasing the taxation paid on benefits is another avenue for reducing costs in a targeted fashion in those countries where the income tax structure is progressive. This could be achieved by removing the favourable tax treatment of pension payments where that exists, or placing a surcharge on pension income, as is the case in New Zealand.

More progressive targeting of flat-rate benefits to those with low incomes is another avenue followed by several countries. For example, Canada has recently announced a more highly targeted system based on family income. It uses the mechanism of a refundable tax credit.

Many countries (including Canada, Denmark, Finland, the Netherlands and Sweden) enhance the transparency of their pension systems by funding the present targeted income assistance programmes for the elderly from general taxation. Others (including France, the United Kingdom and the United States) have kept the funding and administration of both types of public pensions more integrated, perhaps in some cases fearing that making the cost of targeted benefits more easily identifiable might put them under threat.

C. Market responsiveness and active ageing challenges

Market responsiveness and active ageing challenges are discussed in Chapter 4 where pensions changes are examined with other reforms that would work in the direction of extending work later in life on a gradual basis and that would remove obstacles to work and learning that face older people.

There are several changes in pension policy that could lead to a more positive use of individual capabilities, contribute to improving labour market performance, and potentially, to a better standard of living for everyone. As life expectancy increases, if people also are living longer *and* healthier lives, there is a potential loss of national productive capacity if all of the extra years of life are spent in leisure activities. Pension policy could provide important signals that changes in lifetime work patterns are needed – not only to constrain pension cost increases, but also to enhance active ageing.

Changing the "standard" age of entitlement to retirement benefit could be one important signal. However, as noted, such a measure will not increase the *effective* retirement age unless accompanied by other changes – particularly with respect to the labour market. Other areas for pension reform that are discussed in Chapter 4 are actuarial adjustments for people who do not leave at the standard age, the use of partial pension whereby people receive a partial pensions and work part-time, earnings rules, and the role of private pensions in retirement decisions.

Pension reform also can effect the economy through the considerable influence of private pension funds in the functioning of the capital market and in the way in which pension revenues are raised. These topics are discussed in Chapter 5.

D. Balancing individual and collective responsibilities

When the earnings-related public pension schemes (or earnings-related segments of public schemes) were established in their present form in the years following the Second World War, they were designed to combine individual and collective responsibilities. Although contributions were used directly to pay for benefits of those who were already retired, benefits received by individuals were linked to their own contribution record: the schemes were designed so that individuals would earn their pensions by building up a satisfactory contribution record.

This general principle left a great deal of latitude in settling the details. As a result, in some countries the pensions "earned" in this way were way out of line with contributions paid for most contributors – and so were way out of line in aggregate. With the maturation of the systems, the slow-down in economic growth and ageing populations, these schemes now need to be reformed. In France, Italy and Sweden, the earnings-related public schemes are undergoing reforms designed to bring benefits received by individuals closer into line with the contributions they have paid. These reforms have involved many of the measures (increasing retirement age, basing pensions on lifetime instead of final year earnings, changing indexing rules) which were mentioned above.

While in practice it is often hidden by a redistributive flat-rate component of the benefit formula, pay-as-you-go systems can achieve a close relationship between contributions paid and benefits received for each cohort of retirees. Thus, there is no need to abandon established systems to achieve this aim. Of course, in a pay-as-you-go system, the relationship will not necessarily be the same for different cohorts who will experience different "implicit" rates of return to their contributions.[3] However, since individuals cannot change their cohort, this does not detract from the ability of pay-as-you-go systems to ensure that individuals' pensions reflect their own contributions.

Large fluctuations in pension contribution rates can be smoothed out by having the scheme depart from strict pay-as-you-go principles and build up a financial reserve over time: this was done in the past in Canada and Sweden, and the US is still building up a reserve of this sort. But while such measures bring future contribution increases forward, they do not, in themselves, change to any appreciable extent the relationship between contributions paid over a lifetime and benefits received.

In some OECD countries, the earnings-related component of the national pension system is not financed on a pay-as-you-go basis. Rather, each industry or employer accumulates a fund out of which benefits are paid. Such funded occupational schemes can be integrated with each other according to national rules (as in Finland) but are usually more autonomous. In Japan and the UK, employers who offer such schemes can "opt out" of the public earnings-related pay-as-you-go scheme. For such schemes to remain in balance, aggregate contributions and the income earned on those contributions must be equal to aggregate benefits paid. Capitalised systems like this have the clear advantage of making explicit and transparent the funding needed to meet future pension payments. However, there is no necessary relation between the contributions paid on behalf of individuals and the benefits they receive. This will particularly be the case for schemes in which benefits are based on final salaries (rather than average salaries over the contribution period) or where benefits are "integrated" with a public flat-rate pension with a view to ensuring the same *aggregate* replacement rate for all participants.[4]

Schemes in which benefits are not clearly and transparently related to contributions could have complex and potentially undesirable incentives built into them. Where benefits are determined by rather abstract rules based on career paths, there can be distortions in responses to market signals. A particular example of this, discussed above and in Chapter 4, is the tendency of some public and occupational schemes to bias the retirement decision towards early retirement, a tendency which is a serious threat to the viability of public pension schemes.

The reforms mentioned above in pay-as-you-go systems have attempted to address this problem by tying benefits more closely to contribution records. However, the implicit "rate of return" on contributions will be tied to wage rate changes and to changes in total employment – and the latter might well be negative in the future. Thus in present circumstances, individuals are likely to experience a return to their pension contributions which will be substantially inferior to the returns available in financial markets from individual savings.

In the light of these features of public pension systems, and of the high rates of return available in financial markets, there has been a growth in individual savings dedicated to retirement provision. In so-called "defined-contribution" occupational schemes, the major part of – or all of – the contributions to these savings are paid directly by employers on behalf of their workers. In countries with universal earnings-related pension systems, such individual savings supplement the public scheme. However, in Australia (which never implemented a public earnings-related pension) a compulsory system of individualised retirement savings funds has been established, and in Mexico a scheme of this type is largely to replace the earnings-related public scheme. In the UK, individuals can choose to opt out from both the state earnings-related pension scheme and the occupational scheme offered by their employer if they subscribe to a suitable personal pension plan.

Individualised retirement savings funds ensure an explicit relation between contributions and benefits, and may provide better labour market incentives than schemes (both public and occupational) which do not have this feature. However, the pensions received will depend on the savings instruments available and the return received. In all countries which have instituted such systems, the choice of savings instruments is limited: the extent to which flexibility should be allowed is a matter of considerable debate. If small accounts are confined to "safe" bank instruments, the rate of return will be lower than for larger accounts. They thus replace the political risk – that public schemes will promise more than future generations will be able to afford – with the market risk that investments will return less than is initially anticipated.

Taxation of contributions and of investment returns for capitalised schemes is generally deferred in whole or in part until benefits are received. This means tax payment is deferred for up to 40 years, and in a progressive tax system the total tax levied on benefits in retirement is likely to be less than the tax forgone when the recipient was in a higher tax bracket. These timing issues make the measurement of the cost to public budgets of this tax deferral difficult. Nonetheless, any assessment of the overall cost of alternative pension arrangements needs to include the relative impact of tax concessions and any (eventual) reductions in public pension liabilities

In countries with well-designed pay-as-you-go systems, there may be less interest in exploring more radical alternatives. Much debate has concerned the large benefits relative to contributions they provided in the early years after they were established. The plans are now largely mature and this debate is mainly of historic interest. While earnings-related pay-as-you-go schemes have flaws – including the misunderstandings they produce that were referred to at the outset of the chapter – incremental reform may be preferred to the large transitional costs associated with introducing entirely new schemes. Action on many key reforms, such as increasing the age of entitlement to benefits, does not require a change in basic structures.

In any consideration of pension reform, the starting point should be how best to attain the basic goals of pension systems – fiscal sustainability, increasing national savings and investment performance, active ageing, income security for the disadvantaged, stability in the pension contract, personal responsibility and transparency. The best way to achieve these goals will depend on the structures already in place in a particular country, and their current mutual consistency and conformity with the goals. Changes in basic structure can have major effects economically, socially and politically. The costs, as well as the benefits from a new regime, will inevitably influence the choice of reform path.

E. Conclusion: directions for reform

Population ageing creates unavoidable strains on the retirement income system, the costs of which must be borne mainly by those who are now under the age of 40.

The chapter concludes that the easiest way for that cost to be born is through a gradual increase in the age of entitlement to retirement benefit, with flexibility in the work-to-retirement transition. This must be part of a larger package of steps designed to provide appropriate work opportunities for older workers. This larger strategy will, if successful, simultaneously meet a range of fiscal, market responsiveness and social goals.

A second conclusion is that there may be some, albeit limited, scope for cutting pensions of present retirees and those close to retirement, preferably through a targeted approach. This approach would maintain pensions for those with a lower income, while placing more of the adjustment burden on those better off. Even this approach however, would need to be phased in gradually unless there is to be a loss of confidence in the stability of the pension contract.

The precise reforms that are undertaken will depend on the direction that a country wishes to take in the evolving balance between individual and collective responsibilities. Public confidence in the pension contract would be strengthened by a clear statement of longer-term directions and by shorter term reforms that were seen to be moving towards longer-term goals. However, in the absence of a clear consensus on long-term directions, it will be important to find a process such that the debate does not delay immediate reform, especially in the announcement of increased age of entitlement to benefit. Decisions here are needed very quickly to provide the lead time needed for labour market patterns and individual expectations to adjust before the worst impacts of population ageing are felt, early in the next century.

Chapter 3

HEALTH AND LONG-TERM CARE

A. Overview

Ageing populations present large challenges to systems of health and long-term care, particularly in the case of long-term care where changes are needed in both the kind of service that is provided and in financing mechanisms. In terms of the framework for an ageing reform strategy set out in Chapter 1, there are important effects on the fiscal, active ageing and individual/collective balance dimensions.

The *fiscal effects* are the result of a gradual increase in health problems among people as they get older. In addition, there is a heavy increase in health care costs in the year or two preceding death: in some countries one-half of all health care-expenditures occur in the last two years of life. While the precise balance between these two factors is not fully understood, the combined result is that, with ageing populations, there is a heavy concentration of health problems and long-term care costs among older people, particularly the very elderly.

A number of scenarios are used to project the fiscal impacts of ageing and a number of options are presented that would moderate cost increases. However, unless there is some new medical breakthrough in the chronic care area – that would, for example, reduce the duration of dementia – cost increases appear inevitable as a result of the increased need for dependent care among the very old.

Market responsiveness effects are less direct, mainly resulting from improved health among older workers, resulting in a more flexible workforce and less cost to employers and public budgets.

The effects on *active ageing* result from the heavy concentration of health problems among the very elderly. Personal health care expenditure increases only moderately before the age of 60 when mortality is still relatively low. After this age, average health expenditures grow steeply. Preliminary estimates indicate that per capita expenditures around age 70 are twice the average, peaking to four times higher for those aged 80 and above. The concentration of long-term care use among the very elderly is even more dramatic.

In other words, the health characteristics of most people in their 60s and on into their 70s are broadly similar to the rest of the adult population. The stereotype that closely links ageing with infirmity is unfounded. There are enormous health variations within each older age group ranging from persons with hardly any impairment to persons with severe disability.

Being sick and limited in life choices is the antithesis to active ageing. The fact that most older people are reasonably healthy is a sound reason for pursuing active ageing policies including removing barriers to work and learning among people once they pass the age of 65. With the large growth in the number of very old people, dependent care for the frail elderly becomes, in effect, a stage of life that must be recognised by existing public policy. The chapter describes the approaches that countries are taking to develop new solutions.

The effects with respect to *balancing individual and collective responsibilities* are, again, in the area of chronic care for the frail elderly. Reform strategies must recognise that long-term care is a normal risk in society, whose financing requires some form of collective risk-pooling mechanism. And those mechanisms must take into account the major costs, such as long-term nursing care, as well as the more minor costs that now tend to be covered in a more comprehensive way. At present, most of these risk-pooling mechanisms are in the public rather than in the private sector.

B. Health care

Age and health care consumption

The spending increases associated with ageing are particularly steep for institutional care services such as acute hospital care and nursing home care. The increases are less pronounced for consultations with physicians, pharmaceuticals, medical appliances and other ambulatory services. For dentistry there is an early peak around the age of 60 with steady decreases beyond this age.

Where data on non-institutional care expenditures are available for the very elderly, per capita cost-profiles reach a plateau from ages 75 to 79 years, with declines often observed after that age (excluding, of course, the high costs of nursing homes and other long-term care services). More investigation is needed to understand the reasons why this is so. According to a study from the United States, there seems to be an individual age limit for use of certain types of medical high technology.

Costs per service for older people – including a variety of services such as days in hospitals or medical prescriptions – are lower than the average for the population as a whole. However, these lower costs per service are more than offset by much higher rates of use.

Although the evidence is not complete, women appear to be more susceptible to chronic conditions in later life and thus have higher per capita expenditure than men in the same age group. At the same time, the increase in the cost profile of women is less steep.

Some of the most expensive chronic conditions, like dementia, mainly occur in old age. Alzheimer's disease is listed as the third most expensive disease after heart disease and cancer in the United States. Cost-of-illness studies on age-related diseases, like hip fractures, suggest that these should be priority areas for investment in research and development, as well as for better co-ordination of prevention, cure and rehabilitation. Many changes are underway in the organisation of care for the elderly and the outcomes need to be evaluated.

Difference among countries

Tables 3.1 and 3.2 show newly developed data on health expenditure by age. Table 3.1 shows that per capita expenditure for those aged 65 and over are, on average, two and a half to five times higher than for younger people, with even higher ratios for people age 75 and older. There are also big differences among countries. Institutional disparities, such as the extent of public coverage of long-term care costs, rather than underlying differences in health, account for many of these differences.

Variations among countries are especially marked in nursing home care expenditures where the per capita cost for elderly people is up to 15 times higher than for the rest of the population in some countries. In countries such as Belgium, the Netherlands and

Table 3.1.   **Health expenditures by age group and standardisation of expenditure ratios**

	Per capita total health expenditures by age group (0-64 = 100)				Share of total expenditures on health in gross domestic product, 1993		
	Year	65-74	65+	75+	(in %) (1)	Age-standardised (in %) (2)	Index (2)/(1)
United States	1987	314	417	522	14.3	14.5	101
Japan[1]	1993	309	479	573	6.6	6.3	96
Germany	1994	234	268	317	9.3	8.7	94
France[2]	1991	220	296	373	9.8	9.5	97
United Kingdom[3]	1993	254	388	559	6.9	6.5	94
Australia	1989	277	404	598	8.6	9.1	106
Finland	1990	281	395	552	8.8	8.6	98
Netherlands	1994	–	442	–	9.0	8.8	98
New Zealand	1994	233	388	616	7.3	7.7	106
Portugal	1991	140	169	214	7.4	7.4	99
Sweden	1990	230	283	343	7.6	7.1	93
Switzerland	1991	255	400	570	9.5	9.1	96
Average	–	250	231	476	–	–	–

1.   Japan: 65-69, 65+, 70+.
2.   France: 60-69, 60+, 70+.
3.   United Kingdom: England only.
Source: See notes to Tables 3.1 and 3.2.

Table 3.2. **Concentration of total health expenditures on older people, 1993**

	Age group 0-64		Age group 65+		Age group 75+	
	Population (in %)	Expenditures (in %)	Population (in %)	Expenditures (in %)	Population (in %)	Expenditures (in %)
United States	87.3	62.8	12.7	37.2	5.4	20.7
Japan[1]	86.5	57.1	13.5	42.9	8.7	33.1
Germany	84.9	67.7	15.1	32.3	6.5	16.5
France[2]	80.4	58.6	19.6	41.4	–	–
United Kingdom[3]	84.4	58.0	15.6	42.0	6.8	27.1
Australia	88.5	65.5	11.5	34.5	4.5	20.1
Finland	86.2	61.5	13.8	38.5	5.7	22.1
Netherlands	86.9	60.1	13.1	39.9	–	–
New Zealand	88.7	67.0	11.3	33.0	4.6	21.2
Portugal	86.3	64.1	13.7	35.9	5.4	18.7
Sweden	82.5	62.2	17.5	37.8	8.1	21.4
Switzerland	85.7	60.1	14.3	39.9	6.5	26.0

1. Japan: 0-64, 65+, 70+.
2. France: 0-59, 60+, 70+.
3. United Kingdom: England only.
Source: See notes to Tables 3.1 and 3.2.

SOURCES AND NOTES FOR TABLES 3.1 AND 3.2

Total health expenditures are taken form the OECD Health Data information system. Per capita expenditure by age has been calculated on the basis of the sources listed below. Only the sources for the latest year available are cited. For many countries, health expenditure data by age group are not part of standard data collection and different methodologies were applied in the estimates. In some countries, only a regional or institutional sub-sample of the population was available. The estimates calculated for single countries typically have to rely on data obtained from different sources, *e.g.* hospital days by age groups and average costs per day or household surveys on private consumption for health care. In some cases, data obtained for different years were combined in the estimates. In comparing health expenditure by age groups among countries, these qualifications should be kept in mind.

United States

Waldo, D.R., Sonnefeld, S.T., McKusick, D.R. and Asrnett, R.H., III (1989), "Health Expenditure by Age Group, 1977 and 1987", *Health Care Financing Review,* 10(4), 111-120, Summer 1989.

Japan

Ministry of Health and Welfare (1994), National Medical Expenditure Estimates.

Germany

Secretariat's estimates on the basis of risk profiles applied in the risk equalisation formula of statutory health insurance (Gesetzliche Krankenversicherung, GKV). Therefore, data cover only public expenditure.

France

Mizrahi/Mizrahi (1993*), Influence de l'âge et du grand âge sur les dépenses médicales*, Biblio. No. 953, CREDES, Paris.

United Kingdom

Department of Health (personal communication). Data refer to England only (fiscal years).

Australia

Goss, J., Eckermann, S., Pinyopusarerk, M. et Wen, X. (1994), "Health Expenditure on the Aged. Will it Break the Bank?", Paper presented at the ANU Public Policy seminar, Australian Institute of Health and Welfare. Data refer to fiscal years.

Finland

Häkkinen, U., Louet, S. and Salonen, M. (1995), *Terveydenhuoltomenot vuonna 1990 ikä – ja sukupuoliryhmittäin* (Manuscript in Finnish), National Research and Development Centre for Welfare and Health (NAWH), Helsinki.

The Netherlands

Ministerie van Volksgezondheid, Welzijn en Sport (personal communication). Expenditure for "Bejaardenoorden" (homes for elderly) are not part of health care in the definition of OECD health expenditure accounts and where excluded from the data provided by the Ministry.

New Zealand

Ministry of Health (personal communication). Data refer to fiscal years.

Portugal

Departamento de Estudos e Planeamento da Saude (DEPS), Ministerio da Saude, National Health Survey, Northern Region, 1991. The Northern Region is taken as a rough proxy for the whole country.

Sweden

Ministry of Health and Social Affairs (personal communication). Data refer to Malmöhus county only.

Switzerland

Bundesamt für Sozialversicherung. Data refer to one major sickness fund and are therefore only a rough proxy for the whole country.

Formula for age-standardisation in Table 3.1:

Health expenditure can be calculated as a sum of the products of age-specific per-capita expenditure multiplied by the number of persons in each age-group. Age-standardised health expenditures were calculated in Table 3.1 by replacing each country's age structure by an average age structure of OECD countries (an unweighted average was chosen). For data on health expenditure, see *OECD Health Data 96*.

Germany, where only minor parts of long-term care for the elderly are included in public health insurance schemes, expenditures for those 65 and over are from two and a half to three times larger than for those under age 65. In Australia, and Finland, for example, comprehensive care for the elderly is included in their public health care systems and expenditure ratios are four to five times higher.

Not surprisingly, expenditure patterns vary across countries not only because of institutional factors but also because of differences in country age-profiles. Table 3.1 shows age-standardised health expenditures, *i.e.* they assume each country has the same age structure as the OECD average. After standardisation, non-European countries with "younger" populations such as Australia, New Zealand and the United States spend

55

comparatively more, while European countries, such as Sweden and Germany, with a higher proportion of elderly, spend relatively less than without standardisation.

The importance of generational effects

Analysis of the use of health care is based on historic patterns. This tends to underestimate the extent of changes that may affect the health of future older populations. The post-war baby-boom generation that will be very old in 2030 is different from the octogenarians of today. That generation will be better educated, better informed about healthy lifestyles, and better prepared to live independent lives compared with their parents and grandparents. In addition, women are much more autonomous today and participate increasingly in paid work. Each of these factors is an important determinant of future health. This suggests that the baby-boom generation may reach old-age in far better health, on average, than did their predecessors.

The optimistic prospect of a healthy future for the baby-boom generation is damped by the problems faced by the ageing of ethnic minorities and prospects of a growing health divide. There is evidence that not only a socio-economic gradient in health exists but that the scale of income differences within a society is related to average life expectancy and population health.

Only recently have the special needs of ageing immigrants been recognised. There are signals that their integration into the care system for the elderly in a host country will be substantially hampered by, for example, cultural and language differences. These are new challenges to health and long-term care services.

Health expectancy and future costs

Conventional indicators of the health of a population include fatality rates, cause-specific mortality, and life expectancy. However, such measures do not capture the implications of changes in functional health status which are not life threatening. For example, the evidence is not clear whether increased life expectancy reflects in part the prolongation of chronic illness especially among the very elderly, or an increased portion of life lived in relatively good health. There is evidence in some countries that the severity of dysfunction or disability may be declining.

Better evidence about the linkages among mortality, health, dysfunction and ageing would be useful in measuring the effects of changes in health policy and of medical interventions. It would allow better understanding of the reasons underlying differing health trends across countries. And it would allow the construction of better health and long-term care cost estimates in light of ageing populations.

Another uncertainty in projecting future costs is caused by the difficulty in predicting the evolution of health care technology and productivity. If per capita treatment costs rise faster than GDP, as they have done in the past, total health care costs will be higher, even if there is no ageing effect. However, if per capita treatment costs can be reduced below the rate of growth in GDP, demographic pressures from health care will be greatly reduced.

To illustrate the range of uncertainty surrounding the projection of public health care expenditures, six alternative scenarios are presented in Table 3.3. These scenarios are in two groups. The first group of scenarios are calculated by multiplying per capita public expenditure on health by the total number of elderly people. This assumes that as people grow older they consume more health care. These scenarios capture two demographic effects, the increase in the numbers of people becoming elderly and their increased life expectancy. The second group of scenarios are calculated by multiplying per capita expenditure on public health care by the number of deaths among the elderly population. This assumes that consumption of health care is concentrated in the period immediately before death and that as life expectancy rises, an increased portion of life is lived in good health. For most countries, the first group of scenarios generates higher total health care costs, because of the rapid increase in numbers of elderly. Japan, however, shows a different pattern, because its demographic trends mean that it experiences a high number of deaths as the elderly population peaks around 2020. For both groups of scenarios, three alternative assumptions about the growth in expenditure on health relative to GDP were applied. In scenarios where growth in expenditure on health care treatment is assumed to be slower than GDP, overall public expenditure on health care would also be lower, while the reverse holds for the scenarios where growth in treatment costs is faster than GDP.

Reforms of health care systems

Health systems in OECD countries have undergone reforms that will help to moderate the cost effects of ageing populations. Although not always motivated by population ageing, these have favourably affected the delivery and financing of care for the aged. Therefore, continuing efforts to improve the efficiency and effectiveness of health care systems are an important element in responding to ageing populations.

The emphasis of the reforms in the late 1970s was on efficiency, with the aim of restraining the growth of public expenditures on health care. In the late 1980s and early 1990s, there was a wave of structural reforms with a more complex set of motives, including greater effectiveness and greater empowerment of consumers. Global budgets were introduced in some countries along with measures to cap the costs of hospitals, ambulatory care and the purchase of medical goods. Investments in new facilities slowed down and the number of acute-care beds declined. During the period 1983 to 1989, health expenditure as a per cent of GDP for the OECD area remained stable, with limited measured effects on the quality of care.

The second wave of reforms attempted to separate financing from delivery – to have the money follow the patient. This encourages competition among providers to attract patients by offering better service and more effective treatment for a given cost.

Recent reforms emphasise the need for a more rational mix of programmes for different age groups. There is also pressure to achieve more with fewer resources. Earlier reforms were mainly aimed at maintaining stable resource levels.

Table 3.3. **Projected public health care costs in 2030**[1]

As a per cent of GDP

	Health treatment cost growth rates[2]	Public health care costs in 1995	Projected public health care costs in 2030 assuming costs depend on	
			number of elderly	number of deaths
United States	1% slower	6.1	5.2	
	Same rate	6.4	8.2	6.9
	1% faster	11.0	9.3	
Japan	1% slower	4.7	5.4	
	Same rate	4.9	6.3	7.2
	1% faster	8.4	9.7	
Germany	1% slower	5.6	5.5	
	Same rate	6.2	7.8	7.4
	1% faster	10.1	10.0	
France	1% slower	6.6	6.1	
	Same rate	7.0	8.9	8.3
	1% faster	11.9	11.1	
Italy	1% slower	6.0	5.7	
	Same rate	6.4	8.1	7.7
	1% faster	10.8	10.4	
United Kingdom	1% slower	5.2	4.6	
	Same rate	6.0	7.0	6.2
	1% faster	9.4	8.3	
Canada	1% slower	7.6	6.9	
	Same rate	7.4	10.3	9.3
	1% faster	13.8	12.5	
Australia	1% slower	5.6	4.6	
	Same rate	5.8	7.6	6.2
	1% faster	10.2	8.3	
Austria	1% slower	7.7	5.9	
	Same rate	7.4	10.3	8.0
	1% faster	13.8	10.7	
Belgium	1% slower	7.0	5.8	
	Same rate	7.4	9.5	7.8
	1% faster	12.7	10.5	
Denmark	1% slower	5.2	4.3	
	Same rate	5.6	7.0	5.8
	1% faster	9.4	7.8	
Finland	1% slower	7.0	5.5	
	Same rate	6.9	9.4	7.4
	1% faster	12.6	9.9	
Iceland	1% slower	6.8	5.3	
	Same rate	7.4	9.1	7.1
	1% faster	12.3	9.5	

Table 3.3. **Projected public health care costs in 2030**[1] *(cont.)*

As a per cent of GDP

	Health treatment cost growth rates[2]	Public health care costs in 1995	Projected public health care costs in 2030 assuming costs depend on	
			number of elderly	number of deaths
Ireland	1% slower	4.2	3.5	
	Same rate	5.1	5.6	4.7
	1% faster	7.5	6.4	
Netherlands	1% slower	7.3	5.5	
	Same rate	6.7	9.8	7.4
	1% faster	13.2	9.9	
Norway	1% slower	6.9	5.5	
	Same rate	7.6	9.2	7.4
	1% faster	12.4	9.9	
Portugal	1% slower	3.7	3.1	
	Same rate	4.1	5.0	4.2
	1% faster	6.8	5.6	
Spain	1% slower	5.5	4.5	
	Same rate	5.7	7.4	6.1
	1% faster	10.0	8.1	
Sweden	1% slower	5.9	5.0	
	Same rate	6.2	7.9	6.7
	1% faster	10.6	9.0	

1. In projecting these public health cost scenarios, the following methods were used. First the current population and the population projections were split into those under 65 years and those 65 years and over. For some countries, the over 65 years group was split further into those aged between 65 and 74 years and those 75 years and over. Current per capita public health care costs were calculated for each of these groups using recent data. These per capita health costs, adjusted for alternative growth rates in health treatment costs were then applied to the population projections. For the scenarios with constant cost profiles, per capita costs were multiplied by the total number of people aged 65 and over. For the scenarios where costs depend on fatality rates, the per capita costs were multplied by the number of deaths amongst people aged 65 and over.
2. Assuming that per capita health care treatment costs grow by the same rate, 1 per cent slower or 1 per cent faster than real GDP growth.
Source: OECD.

C. Long-term care

Recent trends in long-term care policies

Until recently, few countries had an identifiable policy towards long-term care. Health care in hospitals was frequently extended where necessary to provide long-term stays. Old people's homes provided a refuge for the indigent and frail whose families could not provide for them. Families that did provide care did so without access to services such as respite care, home help and meals-on-wheels. Social policy towards the elderly focused firstly on supporting incomes in old age, and secondly on minimum housing and health standards. The focus has shifted only recently to long-term care, as demographic growth created a large new constituency. As late as 1980, when the OECD hosted a conference on "The Welfare State in Crisis", this issue received little attention in the debates.

However, the remarkable boost in demographic growth in the over-80 group since around 1980 has forced this issue onto the front ranks of the agenda. In this most recent period, a number of common trends in services have been discernible, to a greater or lesser degree, in most OECD countries as they have adapted to this growth. They can be expected to continue in future years until a new balance of services is reached.

Firstly, long-stay wards in general hospitals are not seen as appropriate settings for long-term care. The greater efficiency in acute hospital bed use that has been triggered by new surgical technology has been matched by reductions in long-term hospital beds, other than for severe psychiatric conditions. Since hospitals are among the most expensive forms of long-term care, social and fiscal priorities coincide here.

Secondly, there has been continued expansion of nursing home bed numbers in most countries, as an alternative to hospital-based services. These institutions have become more specialised, catering for an increasingly older and more disabled population with a high need for constant nursing care. Systems of pre-admission assessment have been improved, diverting lesser needs to other services, and systems of reimbursement have reflected the greater differentiation of care provided within nursing homes. The rate of growth recently has been held below demographic growth in a number of countries.

Thirdly, traditional old people's homes, that provide social care to the less handi-capped, are reducing in numbers, in some countries at a rate which suggest they could virtually disappear within a decade or so. They are being superseded by services such as day-care centres and respite care that enable elderly people to remain in their own homes. For those who develop dementia and are at too-great risk if left alone, specialised small-scale hostels for 5 or 6 people are increasingly preferred to larger institutions where experience has shown that the conditions of inmates will deteriorate rapidly.

While the infrastructure of supportive services has grown, earlier hopes that these could divert a significant number of disabled elderly people from expensive nursing homes have been disappointed. There are a number of reasons for this:

- There are many more disabled elderly people already living in the community, and within the scope of new services, than are likely to enter nursing homes. They are all legitimate clients for new services, and "targeting" those most at risk has had only limited success.
- Maintenance at home rests largely on the 24-hour surveillance and support of a family member, not solely on formal services. Family support of elderly people is already extensive and unlikely to be able to be further expanded. Indeed, one of the more positive outcomes of home care services has been the greater security for family carers who hitherto received little formal help.

In most countries, therefore, the goal of home and community-based care is now couched in terms of providing better services, at broadly similar overall cost, rather than a low-cost alternative to nursing homes.

A further lesson from experience with long-term care services has been that entry to nursing homes frequently does not occur after a long period of decline in personal functioning but following a sudden loss of faculty with injury or illness, followed by a spell in hospital receiving acute care. Many placements are therefore from the hospital rather than directly from the community. Health services such as post-acute care and rehabilitation may therefore provide a way of preventing long-term institutionalisation, as well as action in community social services. In most OECD countries, these health services have not yet received the priority they deserve, perhaps because of the persistence of a model of ageing as a process of slow and inevitable decline. Their potential to prevent both social and fiscal costs seems considerable.

The OECD countries have now a better understanding of the type of service infrastructure which will be required in a society with many more very elderly people, and of the potential and limitations of such services. There is a considerable degree of consensus emerging around the scenario outlined here. However, there remain considerable and as yet unresolved differences around an equally pressing issue: namely, who will pay for these reforms?

Reforms in long-term care financing

The growing demand for long-term care, especially in the burgeoning nursing home sector, has led to considerable pressures on traditional mechanisms for funding health and social services in the OECD countries. In recent years many countries have considered the options for reform to these financing mechanisms, reforms which in a number of countries have been implemented at a time when fiscal pressures have been severe. This has not made the process of reform any easier: there is no surplus for distribution to new services, and a deliberate and sometimes painful process of trade-off has resulted. The OECD countries face some difficult choices in future years if a new long-term care infrastructure is to be developed that will be capable of supporting the numbers involved.

Use of private long-term care insurance has grown in some OECD countries during the past decade and insurance companies are interested in developing this new growth area. However, there remain a number of significant barriers in the way of a more general recourse to this means of covering this risk, e.g. the cost of the policies, the length of time they must be held before benefits will be paid, and the experience of high drop-out rates from existing policies. Public mechanisms seem likely to have to continue to bear most of the burden. A number of countries have embarked on a significant reform of these mechanisms during the 1990s.

These reforms have tended to fall into two groups, broadly divided by whether the country concerned has a system of tax-funded health and social services or whether it has a mainly social insurance-based health system. In the former group, issues of efficiency and effectiveness for tax outlays have been paramount. In the latter group, identification of new sources of finance for long-term care has been a matter of growing policy debate.

Some of the former group of countries have opted for a system of block grants to cover most long-term institutional and community services, to enable both overall cost control and a supply of services that is more closely related to individual needs. This has entailed moving away from specific subsidies to local governments for nominated services (in the Nordic countries) and away from a social assistance entitlement linked to institutional care (in the United Kingdom) towards a more flexible system of care financing.

This system is sometimes referred to as a capped budget system, but this description is only partially correct. The authorities concerned are free to redirect finance from other services for which they are responsible (*e.g.* in the case of local governments, education, housing; in the case of health authorities, hospital services), but receive a capped grant from central government for which the formula includes elements relevant to long-term care, *e.g.* the number of elderly people in the area. There is therefore flexibility within a wider financial total rather than a long-term care budget cap. However, while long-term care services are not budget capped, neither are they protected from other expenditure pressures. Flexibility has been achieved, but at the cost of some vulnerability of "soft" services in the face of other competing demands.

Several countries with a health and welfare system which is broadly based on a social insurance model have adopted a different approach. In these countries, the lack of insurance coverage for long-term care on a broadly similar basis to other health services has emerged as a major political issue, with strong demands from those at risk (or the following generation) for new forms of coverage. Pressures from long-term care costs falling on other budgets, *e.g.* social assistance budgets or hospital budgets, have also led to demands for new forms of financing. Noteworthy among these developments are:

- Austria in 1993 replaced the existing set of federal and local cash allowances for care with a unified system of long-term care allowances.
- Germany in 1994 legislated for a new branch of social insurance to cover long-term care, and for the necessary new contributions.
- France in 1995 announced an extended system of care allowances, payable to both those in the community and in institutional care, to be introduced in 1997.
- Luxembourg has declared in favour in principle of an extension of funding for long-term care services. A proposed social insurance model is being considered (December 1995).
- In Japan, the Council on Ageing has conducted an inquiry into the options and presented an interim report in January 1996.

It would appear that wider long-term care financing will be a feature of the welfare system in all of these countries by the end of decade, despite current fiscal constraints requiring reforms to other elements in those systems.

The obstacles in the way of long-term care reforms that require new resources should not, however, be underestimated. The example of the United States, where health reform proposals failed to get enacted in 1994, indicates the difficulties to be encountered when fiscal constraints require the politics of trade-off. In many countries, proposing tax and contribution increases may be politically impossible, and, when compensating savings are required for new benefits, those with existing entitlements do not relinquish benefits lightly.

D.   Conclusion: directions for reform

Different approaches to reform apply to health and long-term care. There are mature health care systems in most Member countries. A number of specific changes are therefore proposed to improve the operation of those systems in light of the challenges of an ageing population. In the case of long-term care, where major changes to systems are under way, the proposal takes the form of a general framework to help guide those who are undertaking these more basic structural reforms.

Research and development

There is room for much improvement both from more investment in research and development (R&D) and a reallocation of research towards chronic conditions. It has been estimated that between one and two fifths of health care expenditures lack clinical justification and have unproved or even adverse effects. The figure is likely higher for care of the elderly. There are large variations between countries in medical practice and resource utilisation in care for the elderly that cannot be explained by differences in morbidity. For example, expenditures on pharmaceuticals with unproven or dubious effectiveness is highly concentrated among the elderly. Moreover, not enough is known about the treatment of chronic conditions and the process of mental degradation.

The benefits of further R&D could be significant. For example, even without a cure, a postponement of the onset of Alzheimer's disease by five years could reduce the disease burden by one half. This applies to other chronic conditions in old age such as osteo-arthritis and chronic back pain.

Prevention of illness and the promotion of health

Cost-effectiveness studies have proven the value of interventions like vaccination against influenza and pneumonia in old age and the prevention of home accidents, hip fracture, osteo-arthritis and chronic back pain. Avoidable morbidity, also, includes the adoption of health promotion practices, such as hormonal replacement treatments for menopause which appear to reduce the incidence of bone fractures and other osteo-arthritic therapies.

Improved secondary prevention through screening and periodic examination is effective and inexpensive in some important areas. Two of the most common chronic conditions, diabetes and hypertension, can, if undiscovered, lead to serious complications, disability and increased mortality. Tertiary prevention includes rehabilitation to help elderly people keep or regain active life after injury or in case of chronic conditions and impairment.

Education and training of health personnel

Unfortunately, health providers often receive less education and training in geriatric care than is desirable. The curriculum on geriatric care is typically less than 100 hours in medical education, although around half of all patient-physician contacts are by older people. Moreover, education in geriatrics should be continuous in order to disseminate the latest information.

Goals for long-term care

While health and long-term reforms overlap, long-term care presents a special policy challenge. It is an area that is like to grow rapidly and that is in need of a new approach to delivery and finance. Countries are now exploring many alternatives. No single solution is likely to be best for all countries because of differences in current structures, in fiscal situations and in political priorities. However, proposals can be assessed against a common set of goals that are described below. These do not all point in the same direction and trade-offs will be needed.

The first and most important goal is to treat long-term care as a normal life risk. Findings from such different welfare systems as Sweden and the United States suggest that the probability for someone aged 65 of needing institutional long-term care at some point during their older years is around 40 per cent. This is a significant risk and points strongly to collective risk-pooling mechanisms as being the most efficient solution.

Secondly, available finance should be focused to provide coverage against the most catastrophic costs. Where families are expected to pay for nursing home fees, the financial effect is considerable. If this risk is considered as part of the total health care package, it is by no means obvious that it is a lesser priority than, for example, routine pharmaceuticals, visits to the physician, or regular optical and dental care. Indeed, health financing systems that provide generous help to younger "worried well" people but require high payments when the patient is old and chronically sick could be judged to be failing on a fairly fundamental level.

Thirdly, reform options should aim to create a more balanced delivery system, such that demand is not channelled into particular service options merely because of their availability. In particular, the balance should tilt towards services supporting people in their own home, such as home health care, personal domestic care, meals on wheels and day care services. Currently, public expenditure on long-term care is in all countries overwhelmingly for nursing home rather than home care.

Finally, any new reform system must be affordable in terms of both public and private expenditures. While public willingness to contemplate higher taxes or contributions for social programmes evidently differs between the OECD countries, greater attention needs to be given to the overall societal costs of reform options. Just because expenses fall in the private sector does not mean that society does not incur them, although it may mean that they fall heavily on particular families rather than being pooled across all.

Chapter 4

LABOUR MARKETS

A. Overview

The ageing challenges described in Chapter 1 all point to the desirability of increasing the effective age of retirement – by removing barriers to working later in life, preferably on a gradual basis involving flexible part-time working arrangements. The *fiscal effects* were described in Chapter 2 which assumed that, if ages of entitlement to retirement benefit were raised, people would in fact work longer. Indeed, there would be little point in signalling the need to work longer in the absence of signals that the necessary jobs will be there.

The *market responsiveness* benefits flow from a more flexible workforce and increased labour supply. There is a need for implementing policies that would enhance the responsiveness of labour markets to demographic changes. In so doing, individuals' incentives to work and retire could change, thus paving the way for an increase in the effective age of retirement.

And the choice to work later in life, using flexible part-time arrangements, is of central importance to meeting the *active ageing challenge*. There would be an improved balance of *individual and collective responsibilities* if the means are there for individuals to more easily adjust their retirement decisions to changing personal preferences and economic conditions. Individual choice and security would both be improved, with less need for reliance on remedial programmes.

The burden of supporting an older population over the coming decades will depend crucially on the extent to which the population of working age in general, and older workers in particular, will participate in the labour market. Higher employment rates would indeed reduce the fiscal pressures associated with the financing of pensions and health care, while also increasing real incomes for the population as a whole, thereby contributing to solve the difficult policy trade-off between higher taxes and lower benefits.

There is room in all OECD countries to increase aggregate employment rates. Participation rates of certain categories of workers, such as women, are relatively low in many countries. Unemployment rates are high and rising in most OECD countries. And most OECD countries have recorded a significant trend decline of labour force participation of older workers, notably males (Chart 4.1). Indeed, this latter trend is one of the

Chart 4.1. **Labour force participation rates for male workers aged 55 to 64**

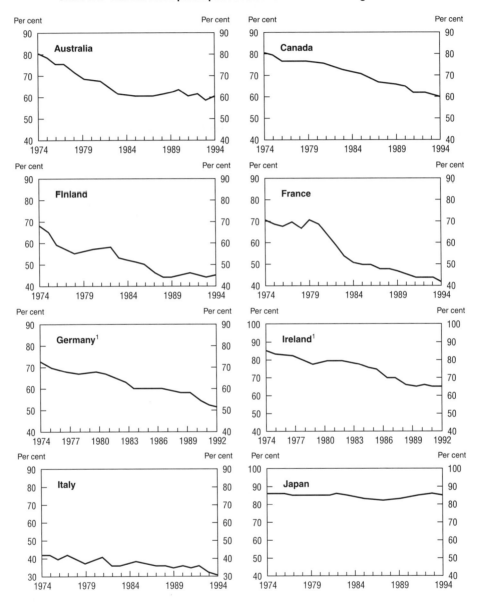

Chart 4.1. *(cont.)* **Labour force participation rates for male workers aged 55 to 64**

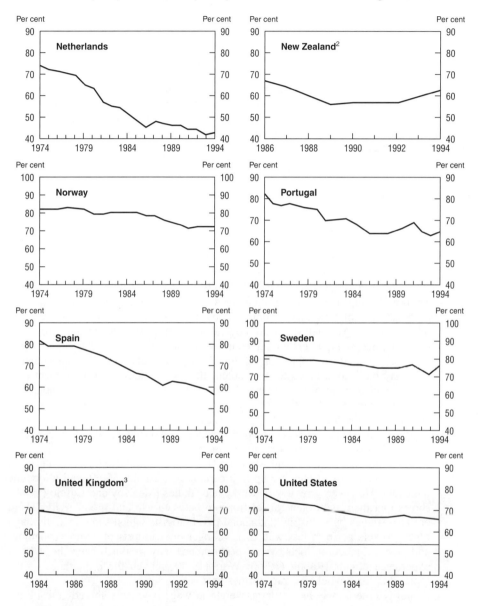

1.   1974-1993.
2.   1985-1994.
3.   1983-1994.
Source: Labour Force Statistics, Part III, September 1995.

most marked features of the recent history of OECD labour markets. It has been argued that one reason for the decline in participation rates of older workers is an increased preference for early retirement. Other factors are likely to be more important, such as retirement policies, social security schemes and demand-side factors.

This chapter begins with a brief discussion of some demand-side factors. It then reviews factors influencing the willingness of older workers to maintain workforce attachment, which include a wide range of government policies. This is followed by a discussion of measures which governments can take to encourage greater lifetime participation by current and future generations of older workers, namely to encourage lifelong learning and more effective active labour market policies. The final section outlines directions for reform.

B. Reasons for low employment among older workers

Factors affecting demand

One possible explanation for falling employment rates is that employers appear to be reluctant to employ or even retain older workers. The reasons for this reluctance are poorly understood, but some of the possible contributing factors may be:

- Skills and competencies of certain older workers may become obsolete, especially in the absence of continuous training. They may therefore be less productive than other workers. An analysis of employers' attitudes in the United Kingdom suggests that many employers are reluctant to hire old-age workers, the main alleged reason being a lack of appropriate skills [Taylor and Walker (1995)]. This perception may have contributed to the implementation of many early retirement programmes targeted at older workers, discussed below, and a marked reluctance to hire older workers. But the perception may not be accurate. This is taken up below under the discussion of lifelong learning.
- Ageing may shape individuals' performance and productivity. The available empirical evidence is, however, mixed. Several studies show a negative relationship. According to Medoff and Abraham (1980), and Ministère du Travail (1994), productivity seems to increase up to a certain age, usually 55-60, and to decline thereafter. However, a review of workplace studies [McEvoy and Cascio (1989)] shows that there is no general relationship between age and productivity. There are also studies by industrial and social psychologists which show that, although older workers perform less well than younger ones in tests of complex memory and physical reaction, their overall performance may be much better because of experience effects [Rabbit (1992); Warr (1992)]. Given the importance of the topic, this issue would warrant further analysis.
- Seniority criteria may have a large weight in wage payments, thereby raising the cost of employing an old-age worker. There is a positive relationship between age and earnings which varies across countries and firms, but seems to be deeply entrenched in OECD economic systems. Chart 4.3 shows patterns of earnings by age for several OECD countries. In the United States, Japan and, to a lesser

Chart 4.2a. **The fall in participation rates of male workers aged 55 to 64 and the rise in total unemployment rates, 1975-94**

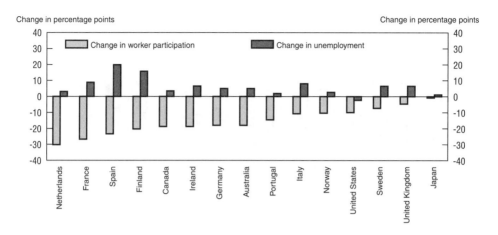

Change in percentage points   Change in percentage points

Notes: Participation: Germany and Ireland, 1993 data; Italy, ages 60-64.
Unemployment: Australia, ages 55 and over; Italy: ages 60-64; Norway, ages 60 and over.
Source: Labour Force Statistics, Part III, September 1995.

Chart 4.2b. **The fall in participation rates and the rise in unemployment rates of male workers aged 55 to 64, 1975-94**

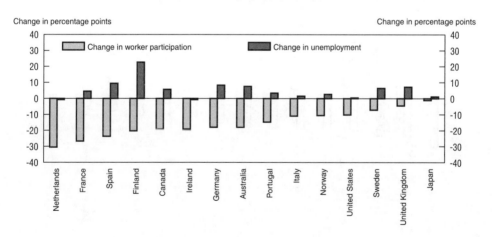

Change in percentage points   Change in percentage points

Notes: Participation: Germany and Ireland, 1993 data; Italy, ages 60-64.
Unemployment: Australia, ages 55 and over; Italy: ages 60-64; Norway, ages 60 and over.
Source: Labour Force Statistics, Part III, September 1995.

Chart 4.2c. **The fall in participation rates of male workers aged 55 to 64 and the rise in total male unemployment rates, 1975-94**

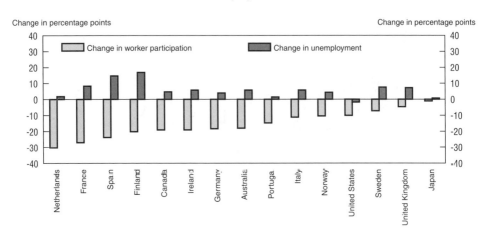

Notes: Participation: Germany and Ireland, 1993 data; Italy, 60-64.
Unemployment: Italy, ages 14-24; Norway and United Kingdom, ages 16-24.
Source: *Labour Force Statistics*, Part III, September 1995.

Chart 4.2d. **The fall in participation rates of male workers aged 55 to 64 and the rise in youth unemployment rates, 1975-94**

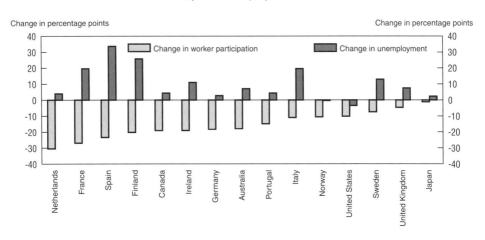

Notes: Participation: Germany and Ireland, 1993 data; Italy, 60-64.
Unemployment: Italy, ages 14-24; Norway and United Kingdom, ages 16-24.
Source: *Labour Force Statistics*, Part III, September 1995.

Chart 4.3. **Age profiles of average earnings**

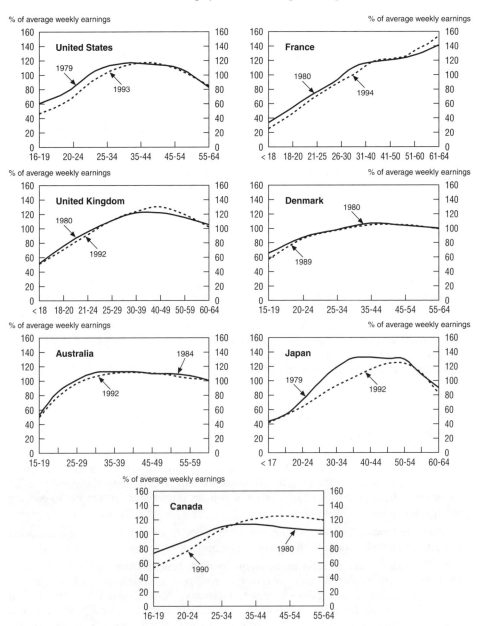

% of average weekly earnings

% of average weekly earnings

% of average weekly earnings

% of average weekly earnings

% of average weekly earnings

% of average weekly earnings

% of average weekly earnings

Source: Direct submission by national authorities.

71

extent, the United Kingdom, earnings flatten out around age 50-55 and decline markedly thereafter. By contrast, in France earnings rise uninterruptedly with age. The age profile of earnings, combined with employers' perceptions about productivity of old-age workers, might inhibit the demand for old-age workers. Even though it is difficult to assess the empirical validity of this view, the issue of how the age profile of earnings is determined is a matter of policy concern.

In principle, the expected changes in the age structure of the labour force that accompany the ageing process should flatten the age profile of earnings over the coming decades, thereby lowering the relative costs of employing older workers. However, the earnings of older workers in large firms may be determined more by their position within an internal labour market than by the balance of supply and demand in the outside labour market. Such practices may improve incentives that foster productivity [Lazear, 1979)]. They may also be an integral part of occupational pension schemes. The issue is therefore how far seniority wage systems will respond to an increase in the relative supply of old-age workers. It is unclear how rapid this process will be and how large an impact it will have on relative labour demands.

Some authors claim that wage systems do adapt to changing demographic patterns. For example, Easterlin (1980) provides evidence for the United States that members of large cohorts suffer reduced lifetime earnings, largely as a result of competition from their peers. However, other authors find no evidence in support of this view. The baby-boom generation should provide a good test case. While some studies, notably for the United States, claim to show that generational crowding did have a negative effect on relative youth earnings, this process should have been reversed since the late 1980s as the baby-boom generations entered the labour market. However, there are very few signs of this expected flattening in age-earnings profiles yet [OECD (1996c)].

Factors affecting the willingness of older workers to participate in the labour market

Individuals may wish to work longer in anticipation of retirement and to have a more flexible transition from work to retirement. However, certain provisions of pension schemes and the presence of early retirement policies often reduce incentives to prolong participation in the labour market.

Early retirement is often encouraged, in the hope that it can improve job prospects for the unemployed, especially the young unemployed:
- For older workers receiving an unemployment benefit, there has been explicit or implicit relaxation of rules governing its receipt (*e.g.* search for work, availability criteria, etc.).[5] Australia, Belgium, Germany, New Zealand and the United Kingdom all have provisions in this area. Italy has also recently introduced a "Mobility Allowance" (effectively an unemployment benefit) as part of the reform to the wage compensation fund (CIG) to help workers on collective layoff whose dismissal is permanent. For older workers, this allowance is paid through

to retirement in regions of high unemployment, and in regions of low unemployment, the maximum duration of benefits can be up to 4 years [OECD (1995b)].

- Many European countries have so-called "unemployment pensions"– which fall under the broader umbrella of early retirement schemes – or special provisions in their unemployment benefit systems that apply to older workers. These unemployment pensions or provisions typically provide extended benefits to long-term unemployed workers – or older workers who have been made redundant – until they reach the standard age of retirement, and subsequently become eligible for a public pension. Countries with provisions in this area include Austria, Belgium, Finland, France, Germany, Italy, the Netherlands, Spain and Sweden (up to 1991) [OECD (1995a); MISSOC (1995)].

- Distinct from special provisions for unemployed older workers are plans that have been introduced in various time periods to allow employed older workers to take early retirement prior to the standard age of entitlement provided they are replaced with unemployed workers, typically youths. In Denmark, about 3 per cent of the working-age population receive this form of benefit [OECD (1995b)]. Other countries which have or had early retirement pensions with a replacement condition include Belgium (since 1976), France (1982-88), Germany (1984-88) and the United Kingdom (1977-88). Although these measures have been phased out in most countries which had them, they may have left behind the idea (both to individuals and employers) that in times of very high unemployment, public pressure could lead to their resurrection. These sorts of plans also tend to be costly because of differences between pension entitlements and unemployment benefits, and through reductions in the labour force and a loss of skilled older workers.

An international comparison suggests that there is no relationship between the fall in participation rates of older workers and unemployment recorded in most OECD countries over the past few decades, suggesting that early retirement programmes fail to reduce unemployment (Chart 4.2). There are several reasons for this failure. First, a withdrawal of old-age workers from the labour market does not necessarily entail a hiring of an unemployed person to fill the resulting job vacancy. The reason is that in sectors/firms where industry-specific human capital is important, many old-age workers may not be easily replaced by new workers. Second, even if these old-age workers could be replaced, they could still look for another job and, eventually, find it. However, social security benefits – a compensation for early retirement – are often sufficiently generous that they discourage active search for a job, depriving the economy of valuable resources. Third, certain provisions of social security schemes may create a high reservation wage for old-age workers. In this context, these workers will have few incentives to adapt to changing labour market conditions, while also perpetuating wage rigidities. Instead of reducing unemployment, forced early retirement may in fact aggravate the problem over the longer run, as early retirement is often financed by higher taxes. More generally, early retirement programmes do not remove the distortions that cause unemployment.

Invalidity and sickness benefits have also been used in many countries as surrogate early retirement schemes, particularly when unemployment rates have been high. This not only affects current flows into (effective) early retirement, it also has an impact on the behaviour of future cohorts of older workers by leading them to expect that they too will be able to leave the labour market earlier than normal and act accordingly, for example by reducing their work effort:

- In many countries, there are significant numbers of older individuals receiving invalidity benefits (IVB) [OECD (1995a, Table 4.6)]. One of the more important factors that pertains to older workers is the use of labour market conditions in determining IVB eligibility. Where these have been used, e.g. in Austria, Finland and Sweden, the outcome is relatively high numbers of older workers in receipt of this benefit. Other countries which have/had labour market provisions for the receipt of IVB include Australia, Germany and the Netherlands. In some cases, when unemployment benefit entitlements are exhausted, IVB have been used as a bridge until a worker reached the standard age of entitlement. Given the increase in numbers of individuals receiving invalidity benefits, however, countries have begun to tighten up eligibility requirements [outlined in OECD (1995a, e)]. These include a tightening up of labour market conditions or their abolition (Australia, the Netherlands, Sweden); the tightening up of the definition of disability (the Netherlands, the United Kingdom) and the introduction of medically verifiable criteria (Sweden); the use of third-party doctors as opposed to a personal doctor (Norway); and where partial disability exists, the expansion of the concept of a "reference job" beyond the previous occupation of the disabled person (the Netherlands). Replacement rates for IVB have also been cut in some countries. On the other hand, IVB replacement rates rose in Sweden, Switzerland and the United States. The net impact on the number of IVB beneficiaries is unclear in those cases where a tightening of eligibility criteria was accompanied by an increase in replacement rates.
- Sickness benefits play an important role in helping workers maintain attachment to the workforce during times of temporary – but in some cases extended – illness. To remove the incentive for the unemployed to claim illness – and use sickness benefits to extend the unemployment spell – many countries have aligned replacement rates for unemployment and sickness benefits. But in some countries – Germany, Austria, Belgium, Finland, Greece, Germany and Italy – sickness benefit replacement rates are higher in the short term; there is evidence in Denmark and Australia that workers transferred from sickness to unemployment benefits, thereby managing to extend benefit periods [Blondal and Pearson (1995)]. There are few data available on the number of older workers taking sick leave. Data reported in the 1991 *Employment Outlook* [OECD (1991a), Table 6.6], however, indicate that workers aged 55 and over, particularly men, have the highest overall absenteeism rate due to illness and injury, but it is difficult to determine whether this reflects health problems or disguised early retirement. Where replacement rates are high, and eligibility conditions relatively lax, as is the case in Sweden, the absenteeism rate is also the highest among the countries surveyed. But countries with relatively low take-up rates, such as Belgium and Greece, have relatively high replacement rates, suggesting that the degree of enforcement of eligibility requirements is an important factor.

Among the pension reform options discussed in Chapter 2, an increase in the *age of entitlement to retirement benefits* is the one with the most immediate impact on the labour market. These proposals could bring work incentives more in line with fiscal concerns. In many cases, the adjustment to pension benefits is not actuarially reduced when public pensions are obtained before the statutory age. As a result, workers may have an incentive to retire earlier. Typically, the reduced early pension can be obtained five years before the standard retirement age. A long-service pension (at full entitlement) also exists in some countries (Austria, Belgium, Germany, Greece, Italy and Luxembourg) usually after 35 to 45 years of pension contributions, reflecting the fact that accrual of additional pension rights has ceased. In 1990, about 13 per cent of older workers in Austria were receiving this benefit [OECD (1992), Table 5.14]. Actuarially reduced pensions typically provide a public pension at an earlier age, but with a considerable reduction in benefit. Even where pensions are actuarially reduced, there may be significant numbers of individuals in receipt, for example over 20 per cent of those aged 60-64 in Canada and the United States. By contrast, numbers are much lower in Finland and Sweden (below 4 per cent of those aged 60-64), but this probably reflects alternative incentives to leave the labour force that are relatively more generous (*e.g.* unemployment pensions in Finland).

Earnings' rules may disadvantage people who work longer than the statutory retirement age, which may explain why the transition from work to retirement is often abrupt. Some public pensions have an earnings rule attached to them so that any earnings above a certain limit may result in a substantial reduction in pension payments, or in effect, high effective marginal tax rates on earned income [*e.g.* see Table 2.17, OECD (1995a)]. The marginal tax rates can be 100 per cent on relatively low levels of earned income, which decrease the incentive to seek work while receiving a pension, or discourage additional work by other family members. This has led some countries, including France and the United Kingdom to abolish these rules, although they still exist in Belgium, Germany, Italy and Spain [MISSOC (1995)]. The majority of workers shift from full-time work to full-time retirement for reasons more related to the incentives present in retirement schemes than to their individual preferences. For example, while some countries (Denmark, Finland, and Sweden) offer reduced pensions in combination with part-time work, the take-up of such schemes has generally been low.[6] Earnings rules and means-testing in either public or private pensions may also limit the incentive to take up part-time work, as might entitlement rules *e.g.* whether it is based on previous income prior to retirement and so on.

Certain features of *private pension plans* may inhibit labour mobility. For instance, pension plans may not be portable, meaning that a shift to another job will entail the loss of pension rights. Moreover, pension plans may require a long vesting period, so that pension rights are lost when a worker quits the firm before the end of the vesting period. Limited portability and long vesting periods are commonly found in defined-benefits' schemes in the United States. Also, limited portability is more of a problem in schemes organised at the company level than in schemes covering a whole sector of economic activity. Company-based schemes are relatively more dominant in Canada, the United Kingdom and the United States while those in Europe are typically industry-wide [OECD (1995e), World Bank (1994)]. These features can help increase workers' attachment to the firm and limit labour turnover, thereby facilitating investment in firm-specific human capital. There is evidence that labour turnover is relatively low in firms that provide pension plans [Gustman *et al.* (1994)]. But they can also entail perverse labour market effects. In particular, it has been pointed out that labour market mobility can be inhibited in the presence of these schemes [World Bank (1994)]. Indeed, workers covered by a non-portable pension suffer a (pension) capital loss when they change jobs. The same holds true for workers who change jobs before vesting in their pension.

Gradual retirement schemes could help improve the labour market participation of older workers. Under these schemes a part-time pension benefit is combined with income from a part-time job. Some countries (Denmark, Finland, the Netherlands and Sweden) allow a combination of part-time work and receipt of a public pension before the standard age of entitlement to a full pension.

The *integration rules* between public and private schemes may be one source of bias. If private benefits are available before the age of access to public benefits, the neutral effects of actuarial reductions in public pensions on the incentive to take early retirement disappear.

C. The role of lifelong learning and active labour market policies

There is clearly a need to adjust skills and competencies to meet the needs of ageing populations. This chapter has emphasised the need to increase employment rates and to raise the effective retirement age in order to offset the fiscal burdens associated with ageing populations. At the same time, the evidence suggests that those who work longer enjoy better health in their old age. The policy conclusion is clear: it is imperative to maintain people in gainful activity longer. In order to achieve this objective, it will be necessary to ensure that education and training policies are adapted to the specific needs of older workers.

In recent discussions, OECD Education Ministers emphasised the need for addressing these issues in the framework of a ''lifelong learning'' approach [see OECD (1996b)]. Effective lifelong learning could help upgrade labour productivity, while also enhancing the adaptive capacity of all workers, thereby contributing to increase the employment levels in OECD countries. The need for a lifelong learning approach will be reinforced by the process of ageing populations, for three reasons:

- First, lifelong learning can facilitate the adjustment of workers' skills and competencies to the needs of the market.
- Second, a lifelong learning approach would also help improve the attachment of old-age workers to the labour market. Younger workers are on average more educated and/or have more access to training programmes than older workers (Table 4.1). As a result, older workers find it more difficult to keep pace with changes in production methods. For instance, some authors argue that unexpected increases in the rate of technological change will raise the likelihood of retirement for older workers [Bartel and Sicherman (1993)]. It is more likely that adapting existing skills will be more fruitful than learning new skills through formal

Table 4.1. **Percentage of the population in four age groups that had attained at least upper secondary education, 1992**

Percentage

	25 to 34	35 to 44	45 to 54	55 to 64
North America				
Canada	81	78	65	49
United States	86	88	83	73
Pacific Area				
Australia[1]	57	56	51	42
New Zealand	60	58	55	49
European Community				
Belgium	60	51	38	24
Denmark[2]	67	61	58	44
France	67	57	47	29
Germany	89	87	81	69
Ireland	56	44	35	25
Italy	42	34	21	12
Netherlands	68	61	52	42
Portugal[3]	21	17	10	7
Spain	41	24	14	8
United Kingdom	81	71	62	51
Other Europe – OECD				
Austria	79	71	65	50
Finland	82	69	52	31
Norway	88	83	75	61
Sweden	85	78	63	46
Switzerland	87	84	77	70
Turkey	21	14	9	5
Weighted mean OECD	72	69	60	48

1. 1993.
2. Of the 25- to 34-years olds a relatively large number are still enrolled in education. Data may therefore be biased downward.
3. 1991.
Source: OECD Education Database.

classroom training given the relatively shorter time to recoup costs (probably even given increased working lives, although this should be considered in a benefit-cost analysis). This implies that training should be offered over the life-cycle so that larger amounts of it are not needed at discrete points in time.
– Third, as discussed above, some authors argue that, irrespective of the skills and competencies, productivity declines after a certain age.

A lifelong learning approach would also have profound impacts on the functioning of labour markets. For instance, the pattern of working time throughout the life-cycle would be modified, as more time would be devoted to learning at all ages *and* workers would retire later. It would also have major implications for human resource management at the enterprise level.

However, a move towards lifelong learning will be a gradual process, since many issues such as financing remain unanswered. In the meantime, there is still the need to help older worker adapt during the transition. In principle, well-targeted active labour market policies (ALMPs) could help address the specific labour market problems of older age workers. But relatively few older workers participate in active labour market pro-grammes at present. There is little evidence on what specific active measures work for older workers in terms of raising their employment and earnings' prospects. Some examples of targeted active measures are worth mentioning however:

- The United Kingdom recently raised the maximum age of access to its "Training for Work" programme for the long-term unemployed from 59 to 63 years to help older workers maintain contact with the labour force [Whitting *et al.* (1995)].
- In Japan, there exist a number of measures to help older workers maintain employment. These include subsidies to employers who extend the employment of workers until the age of 65, subsidies to employers whose workforce contains a specified minimum proportion of older workers, subsidies to employers linked to older workers taking public training courses and public training programmes directed at older workers about to leave at the mandatory retirement age. How-ever, these measures remain small in size and there are no evaluations of their labour market impact [OECD (1995*a*)].
- Wage subsidies to encourage hiring of older workers also exist in Germany, Austria and France [Whitting *et al.* (1995)].

D. Conclusion: directions for reform

a) *Improving policy coherence and taking concerted action*

Reforms that are part of a broader reform strategy are more likely to succeed than those that are introduced in isolation. The forces that lead to reduced work for older workers have deep roots in society and in the culture of enterprises. Solutions will have to involve close co-operation among governments, employers and employee representatives to address many inter-related issues. For example, if the incentives to early retirement in existing pensions schemes are eliminated, there is a possibility that early retirement may still proceed through unreformed routes such as invalidity benefits. Similarly, employers have little to gain in investing in the training of older workers if public programmes, directly or indirectly, subsidise the layoff of older workers in a period of down-sizing.

Policy coherence will be improved, for example, as Member countries implement the wide-ranging strategy to tackle the unemployment problem proposed in the *OECD Jobs Study*. This would improve the employment outlook for all workers, both young and old, and serve to increase the growth rate of OECD economies. The proposals in the following paragraphs, which are consistent with the *OECD Jobs Study*, are likely to be central elements of the ageing reform strategies of most Member countries.

b) Make pension schemes consistent with demographic trends

Public pension schemes should interfere as little as possible with the decisions to work, move to another job or retire. This is not the case in current pension systems as they contain incentives for reducing the working life and not working part-time during retirement. Retirement ages can be raised, at least so that men and women are put on equal footing, and retirement ages can be increased for both men and women as life expectancy increases. Changes in these areas should be phased in over time so as not to affect adversely the incomes of the current generation of older workers, and to allow future generations of older workers to adapt their expectations accordingly.

Increasingly, countries are focusing attention on private pension schemes as a means of encouraging individuals to save for retirement. It is important to stress, however, that such schemes may also create labour market distortions. Defined-benefits' schemes, organised at the level of individual companies, may hamper workers' mobility, while encouraging early retirement. Sector-wide defined-benefits' schemes and defined-contributions' schemes are likely to be somewhat more neutral from the point of view of labour market behaviour. Governments may also consider the possibility of regulating vesting periods and portability provisions, as the complexity of private pension schemes makes it difficult for individual workers to figure out the implications of such clauses.

c) Ensuring smooth transitions from work to retirement

The transition from work to retirement is often abrupt. The majority of workers shift from full-time work to full-time retirement for reasons more related to the incentives present in retirement schemes, and responses by employers to these incentives than to their individual preferences. Earnings rules and means-testing in either public or private pensions may also limit the incentive to take up part-time work as a bridge into full-time retirement, as can entitlement rules *e.g.* whether it is based on previous income prior to retirement, which are particularly common in occupational schemes. This calls for flexibility in working-time arrangements, and the appropriate incentives for both workers and firms to make use of them.

Likewise, the introduction of gradual retirement schemes would help increase the incentives to participate longer in the labour market. Such schemes allow people to receive a partial pension while working part-time.

d) Reforming public benefit entitlements

In some cases, early retirement is a deliberate policy, or is encouraged indirectly through lax enforcement of rules and regulations governing entry into various income sufficient systems. Invalidity benefits and unemployment benefits have been used in many countries, for example, as *de facto* early pensions. If the goal is to increase the incentives to remain longer in the labour force, these provisions need to be modified. Early retirement schemes should be calculated on the basis of actuarial criteria. As for other public benefits such as invalidity and unemployment benefits, they should not be used as a mechanism to promote the early retirement of workers. This not only affects the flows into early retirement at present, but also the behaviour of *future* generations who anticipate to leave the labour market earlier than normal and act accordingly, for example by reducing their saving rate or work effort. The appropriate strategy to change incentives may not always involve cuts in benefit replacement rates; better enforcement of the eligibility criteria of these schemes and/or changes in eligibility requirements could achieve this objective too.

More generally, early retirement should not be used as a mechanism to solve short-term labour market imbalances without full consideration being given to its longer-run consequences, including its impact on the anticipations of future generations of older workers.

Employers are sometimes reluctant to keep old-age workers. This may be due to the effects of seniority rules on wages of old-age workers. It may also be caused by perceived declines in productivity after a certain age. Older workers are sometimes regarded as being less adaptable to technological change than younger ones. It is likely that these fears may be exaggerated and are often a rationalisation for unfounded discrimination against older workers. Some countries have therefore enacted legislation to ban age discrimination in hiring, while others provide similar protection through other legislation. It would be important to evaluate the impacts of such legislation.

e)   Helping old-age workers maintain workforce attachment

The meeting of OECD Education Ministers in January 1996 stressed the framework of "lifelong learning" to upgrade labour productivity and increase the adaptive capacity of all workers [see OECD (1996*b*)]. And for older workers there is also a need to promote workforce attachment by participation in various ALMPs. It would be useful to collect more information on various ALMPs with potential effects on employment of older workers and to increase the knowledge or what works in this area.

Chapter 5

FISCAL EFFECTS, NATIONAL SAVINGS
AND CAPITAL MARKETS

A. Overview

This final chapter concentrates on the fiscal dimensions of the reform strategy described in Chapter 1, especially possible effects on savings, on taxation and on capital markets. Ageing affects many dimensions of the national economy. A pressing concern is its effect on government expenditures, particularly pension and health care costs. Potential savings in education expenditures or in the cost of child benefits are likely to be small by comparison. The fiscal effects of selected pension reform options, as discussed in Chapter 2, combined with different assumptions about changes in several major factors that affect health care costs, as discussed in Chapter 3, have been estimated. The scenarios show a significant worsening of fiscal positions assuming a continuation of current programmes, including announced reforms. However, they also show that there are ways to improve the situation, primarily by reducing programme costs.

Raising contribution rates also could ameliorate the problem of burgeoning public expenditures, but this is not an acceptable solution in most countries. An alternative approach to raising more revenue without increasing contribution rates – broadening the revenue base – is examined. The conclusion is that there is not much room for manoeuvre on this front.

Increased government spending and reduced government revenues result in government "dissaving". The full effect on national saving, however, also depends on the response of private-sector saving to the ageing of populations and the response of private saving to lower government saving. The evidence here is not as clear. Moreover, there are different views about the link between saving and national prosperity. On balance, however, the evidence suggests that population ageing does lead to reduced private saving and, given present policies, to significantly lower national savings.

B. Overall fiscal scenarios

The overall impact of ageing populations on government budget positions can only be assessed within a standard budgetary framework which includes all government expenditures, with the major expenditures which affect the elderly adjusted for demographic change. The approach used and results have been reported in detail elsewhere.[7]

The overall fiscal scenario incorporates the baseline scenario for pension expenditures. This assumes that pension programmes remain unchanged, except for reforms that have already been announced (discussed in Chapter 2). Two main assumptions underlie the scenario for health expenditures: health treatment costs grow in line with GDP and the elderly population consume increasing amounts of health care as they grow older. All other revenues and expenditures are held constant as a per cent of GDP,[8] except for net debt interest payments.

In this illustrative scenario, primary balances, that is, government revenues minus expenditures (excluding net interest payments), deteriorate sharply over time because of the ageing of the population – except in the United Kingdom, as shown in Table 5.1. In most cases, pensions play the major role but rising health care expenditure also plays a part, particularly in the United States, Canada, Austria, Finland and the Netherlands.

General government financial balances, derived by adding together the primary balances and net interest payments, are added each year to the existing stock of net public debt.[9] The rate at which public debt mounts depends on the size of the primary balance and the interaction of debt servicing costs and economic growth.[10] As a rule, if net debt servicing rates[11] remain higher than nominal economic growth rates, public debt will increase – unless the primary surplus is large enough to offset the increase in net interest payments. Because net interest payments rise (fall) if debt is higher (lower), a vicious (virtuous) circle can be created (Chart 5.1).

Overall budget balances and the accumulation of public debt, under alternative assumptions about the relationship between net debt servicing rates and economic growth, are also shown in Table 5.1. The scenarios suggest that, some countries face major problems, with debt mounting to very high levels by 2030: Austria, Japan, the Netherlands and Sweden are particularly badly affected under these scenarios, with debt levels rising to more than 200 per cent of GDP. However, these increases in debt levels reflect not only the demographic pressures, but also the balance between other spending programmes and revenues and the cost of servicing the inherited stock of debt. The "pure ageing effect"– the accumulation of debt due only to demographics – is shown in Table 5.2. Only Ireland is free from demographic pressure. In the majority of countries, the pure ageing effect would add more than 100 per cent of GDP to public debt between 2000 and 2030 alone.

Another way of looking at these fiscal developments is to consider how much taxes relative to GDP would have to rise in order to keep public debt from rising. For a number of countries, tax ratios would have to rise by between 5 and 10 percentage points of GDP. But raising tax ratios is likely to have discouraging effects on working and savings, especially as the countries facing the biggest increases would often be those which already have relatively high tax ratios (see Table 5.3).

Table 5.1. **Fiscal indicators, 1995 to 2030**[1]

As a per cent of nominal GDP

	Primary balance[2]	Interest-growth rate differential constant			Interest rate constant		
		Net interest payments[3]	Financial balance[2]	Net financial liabilities	Net interest payments[3]	Financial balance[2]	Net financial liabilities
United States							
1995	0.4	2.3	−2.0	51	2.3	−2.0	51
2000	0.2	2.1	−2.0	49	2.1	−2.0	49
2015	−0.6	2.5	−3.1	51	3.0	−3.6	54
2030	−3.8	4.8	−8.6	95	7.3	−11.1	115
Japan							
1995	−3.4	0.5	−3.9	11	0.5	−3.9	11
2000	−1.5	1.0	−2.5	25	1.0	−2.5	25
2015	−6.0	4.2	−10.2	102	4.7	−10.7	104
2030	−8.7	13.4	−22.1	317	16.2	−24.9	339
Germany							
1995	−0.6	2.9	−3.5	44	2.9	−3.5	44
2000	−0.1	3.5	−3.6	53	3.5	−3.6	53
2015	−0.2	6.0	−6.2	99	6.1	−6.3	99
2030	−6.6	9.5	−16.1	216	14.5	−21.0	247
France							
1995	−1.6	3.4	−5.0	35	3.4	−5.0	35
2000	1.2	4.0	−2.8	45	4.0	−2.8	45
2015	−0.1	4.4	−4.5	69	5.2	−5.3	73
2030	−4.5	8.6	−13.1	165	11.6	−16.1	193
Italy							
1995	3.4	10.5	−7.2	109	10.5	−7.2	109
2000	3.8	8.1	−4.3	109	8.1	−4.3	109
2015	4.0	10.2	−6.2	123	8.5	−4.5	112
2030	−5.9	14.6	−20.4	234	17.3	−23.2	241
United Kingdom							
1995	−2.8	3.0	−5.7	40	3.0	−5.7	40
2000	0.5	3.6	−3.1	47	3.6	−3.1	47
2015	−0.1	5.8	−6.0	79	5.6	−5.7	79
2030	−1.4	8.4	−9.8	137	10.0	−11.3	144
Canada							
1995	1.5	5.6	−4.2	70	5.6	−4.2	70
2000	4.7	4.6	0.1	60	4.6	0.1	60
2015	4.6	0.8	3.8	3	0.9	3.7	4
2030	−1.0	−1.1	0.1	−27	−1.6	0.6	−29
Australia							
1995	0.0	2.4	−2.4	28	2.4	−2.4	28
2000	1.8	2.1	−0.3	27	2.1	0.3	27
2015	1.3	0.5	0.8	7	0.6	0.7	8
2030	−1.4	0.5	−1.9	10	0.8	−2.2	12
Austria							
1995	−2.7	3.5	−6.2	50	3.5	−6.2	50
2000	0.9	4.5	−3.6	59	4.5	−3.6	59
2015	−2.3	7.8	−10.2	125	7.9	−10.3	126
2030	−7.7	17.4	−25.1	317	20.3	−28.0	340
Belgium							
1995	4.3	8.8	−4.4	128	8.8	−4.4	128
2000	5.9	8.6	−2.8	119	8.6	−2.8	119
2015	5.7	5.2	0.5	78	5.8	0.0	81
2030	−0.5	4.4	−4.9	77	6.2	−6.7	95

Table 5.1. **Fiscal indicators, 1995 to 2030**[1] *(cont.)*

As a per cent of nominal GDP

	Primary balance[2]	Interest-growth rate differential constant			Interest rate constant		
		Net interest payments[3]	Financial balance[2]	Net financial liabilities	Net interest payments[3]	Financial balance[2]	Net financial liabilities
Denmark							
1995	2.0	3.7	−1.8	46	3.7	−1.8	46
2000	3.8	3.1	0.7	37	3.1	0.7	37
2015	1.0	1.0	0.0	12	1.1	−0.1	13
2030	−2.3	2.1	−4.5	34	2.4	−4.7	36
Finland							
1995	−4.3	1.3	−5.6	−7	1.3	−5.6	−7
2000	2.3	0.7	1.5	−5	0.7	1.5	−5
2015	−2.5	−0.5	−2.0	−12	−0.7	−1.8	−13
2030	−8.8	5.6	−14.4	98	6.2	−15.0	99
Iceland							
1995	−1.1	2.3	−3.4	35	2.3	−3.4	35
2000	0.5	2.4	−1.8	34	2.4	−1.8	34
2015	0.0	2.2	−2.2	32	2.3	−2.4	33
2030	−3.3	4.4	−7.7	69	5.8	−9.1	78
Ireland[4]							
1995	1.8	4.2	−2.4	86	4.2	−2.4	86
2000	0.6	3.4	−2.7	74	3.4	−2.7	74
2015	0.6	2.8	−2.3	71	3.7	−3.1	76
2030	0.0	3.7	−3.7	83	5.5	−5.4	102
Netherlands							
1995	1.4	4.7	−3.3	43	4.7	−3.3	43
2000	2.8	4.9	−2.1	45	4.9	−2.1	45
2015	0.0	5.1	−5.1	67	5.4	−5.4	68
2030	−6.0	10.2	−16.2	185	13.3	−19.3	206
Norway							
1995	3.2	0.2	3.1	−26	0.2	3.1	−26
2000	3.2	−0.5	3.7	−37	−0.5	3.7	−37
2015	0.4	−3.8	4.2	−73	−4.2	4.6	−74
2030	−4.7	−3.3	−1.4	−57	−4.6	−0.2	−69
Portugal[4]							
1995	0.6	5.7	−5.1	71	5.7	−5.1	71
2000	1.5	4.3	−2.8	70	4.3	−2.8	70
2015	−0.4	4.9	−5.3	83	5.4	−5.8	85
2030	−5.6	9.8	−15.4	170	12.9	−18.5	192
Spain							
1995	−1.1	5.1	−6.2	50	5.1	−6.2	50
2000	1.5	5.5	−4.0	58	5.5	−4.0	58
2015	0.5	5.6	−5.2	78	6.5	−6.0	82
2030	−4.4	9.7	−14.1	159	13.9	−18.3	191
Sweden							
1995	−5.1	2.9	−8.1	28	2.9	−8.1	28
2000	2.9	3.2	−0.3	32	3.2	−0.3	32
2015	0.2	2.3	−2.2	29	2.4	−2.3	30
2030	−2.7	5.3	−8.0	78	5.7	−8.4	81

1. 1995 and 2000 data correspond to OECD Secretariat's Medium Term Reference Scenario.
2. Surplus (+) or deficit (−).
3. The calculation of net interest payments after 2001 is based on separating the stock of debt into two parts: debt accumulated up until 2000 ("old" debt) and additional debt accumulated from onwards ("new" debt). For the old debt, the net interest payments are derived using the implicit interest rate on the old debt (net interest payments divided by net debt). For new debt, long-term market interest rates are assumed to apply. These were derived by calculating an average projected real interest rate analysed here and then using each country's projected individual inflation rate (in 2000) to calculate the nominal interest rate.
4. Gross financial liabilities for Ireland and Portugal.
Source: OECD.

Chart 5.1. **Impact of different initial primary balances on net debt**
As a percentage of GDP[1]

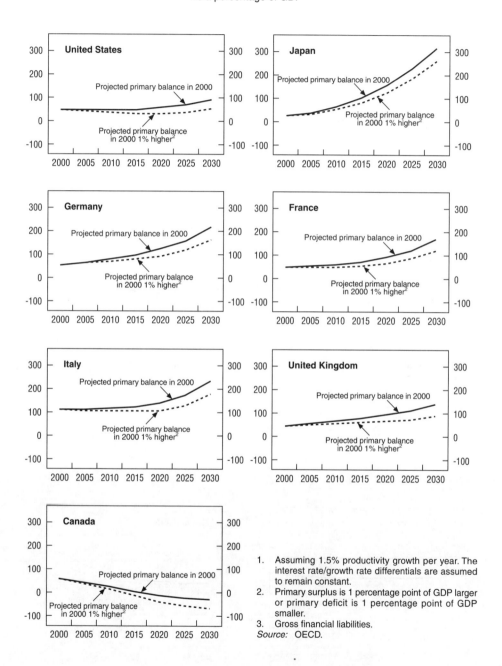

1. Assuming 1.5% productivity growth per year. The interest rate/growth rate differentials are assumed to remain constant.
2. Primary surplus is 1 percentage point of GDP larger or primary deficit is 1 percentage point of GDP smaller.
3. Gross financial liabilities.
Source: OECD.

Chart 5.1. *(cont.)* Impact of different initial primary balances on net debt
As a percentage of GDP[1]

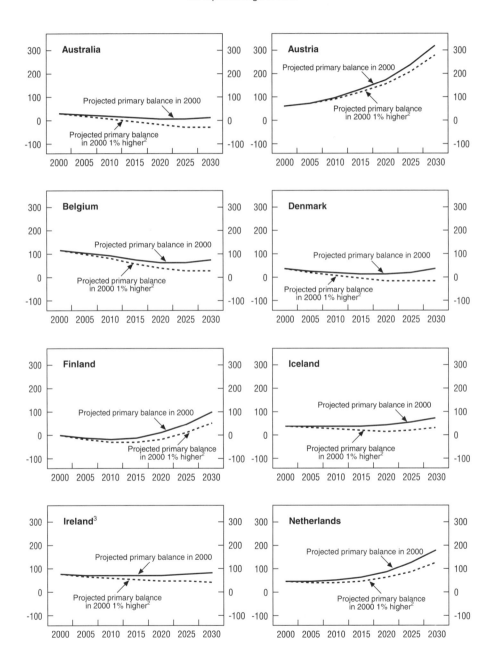

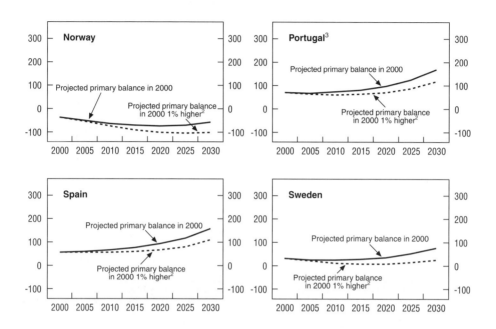

Another policy approach that would improve the overall primary balances is the reduction of non-age-related expenditures. The sooner this is done, the larger the impact it would have because of the vicious/virtuous effects of debt dynamics. If, for example, primary expenditures were one per cent of GDP lower every year from 2000 onwards than in the baseline, it would make a difference of around 30-50 percentage points of GDP to the level of debt by the year 2030.

While faster economic growth would be helpful, it would only partially alleviate the problem because of the way in which income-related pension expenditures tend to move in line with economic growth.[12] In any case, it is far from clear how much the government can do to achieve a sustained, non-inflationary, increase in economic growth rates (see Table 5.3).

In practice, governments pursue a mix of strategies depending on country circumstances. These include reducing non-age related expenditures, review of taxes and pension contributions as discussed below, various age-related reforms discussed in Chapters 2, 3 and 4, and other policies directed to increased economic growth and employment.

Table 5.2. **Pure ageing effects on net financial liabilities, 2000-2030**[1]

As a per cent of GDP

	Interest rate constant	Interest-growth rate differentials constant
United States	44	41
Japan	190	180
Germany	45	42
France	62	60
Italy	109	103
United Kingdom	27	26
Canada	39	38
Australia	37	34
Austria	171	162
Belgium	42	41
Denmark	124	120
Finland	213	199
Iceland	41	38
Ireland	2	2
Netherlands	142	132
Norway	135	127
Portugal	110	102
Spain	66	61
Sweden	117	114

1. The pure ageing effect is estimated by measuring the accumulation of net financial liabilities resulting only from the change in primary balances from 2000 to 2030. Apart from demographic effects primary balances are held constant at their levels in 2001.

Source: OECD.

C. The revenue base

The projections above show that if pension programmes are not changed, the tax or contribution rate required to finance transfers to the elderly will rise considerably. As the number of workers per pensioner falls, typically from around 2.5 to 1.5, a pension of 60 per cent of average earnings would require an increase in contributions from 24 to 40 per cent of earnings.[13] Governments are already concerned about the high tax burden on labour, which may reduce individuals' incentives to work and firms' incentives to hire them. Social security contributions increased from an average of 4.9 to 10.2 per cent of GDP in OECD countries between 1985 and 1993. They now make up 27 per cent of total revenues, compared with 19 per cent in 1965 (OECD, 1995g).

Two sets of policies designed to minimise the rise in contributions were outlined in Chapter 2: the first set aims to increase the ratio of workers to pensioner, for example, by prolonging working life and reducing use of early retirement programmes; the second set

Table 5.3. **Increase in tax/GDP ratios required to keep net debt constant**[1]

As a per cent of GDP

	Interest rate constant	Interest rate-growth rate differentials constant
United States		
2005	−0.3	−0.3
2015	1.4	1.1
2030	5.3	4.6
Japan		
2005	3.5	3.5
2015	6.9	6.7
2030	9.6	9.5
Germany		
2005	2.8	2.8
2015	2.6	2.5
2030	9.7	8.8
France		
2005	0.8	0.8
2015	2.9	2.5
2030	7.1	6.6
Italy		
2005	1.8	1.8
2015	−0.4	0.4
2030	11.4	10.2
United Kingdom		
2005	1.7	1.7
2015	1.8	2.0
2030	3.5	3.1
Canada		
2005	−3.2	−3.2
2015	−2.4	−2.8
2030	3.6	2.7
Australia		
2005	−1.3	−1.3
2015	−0.5	−0.7
2030	2.4	2.0
Austria		
2005	3.8	3.8
2015	7.3	7.2
2030	15.4	15.0
Belgium		
2005	−2.0	−2.0
2015	−0.9	−1.5
2030	5.9	4.7

Table 5.3. **Increase in tax/GDP ratios required to keep net debt constant**[1] *(cont.)*

As a per cent of GDP

	Interest rate constant	Interest rate-growth rate differentials constant
Denmark		
2005	–1.9	–1.9
2015	0.5	0.4
2030	3.8	3.7
Finland		
2005	–1.4	–1.4
2015	2.7	2.7
2030	8.8	8.9
Iceland		
2005	–0.3	–0.3
2015	0.7	0.6
2030	4.3	3.9
Ireland		
2005	–0.3	–0.3
2015	1.0	0.3
2030	1.8	1.1
Netherlands		
2005	0.8	0.8
2015	3.1	2.9
2030	9.0	8.5
Norway		
2005	–2.7	–2.7
2015	–0.7	–0.5
2030	3.8	4.1
Portugal		
2005	0.5	0.5
2015	2.2	2.0
2030	8.2	7.4
Spain		
2005	0.9	0.9
2015	2.3	1.9
2030	7.4	6.6
Sweden		
2005	–0.6	–0.6
2015	1.4	1.3
2030	4.0	3.9

1. Increases in tax/GDP ratios required to keep net financial liabilities constant as a per cent of GDP from 2000 onwards, assuming fiscal consolidation takes place between now and 2000, according to the path indicated by the OECD Secretariat's Medium Term Reference Scenario, "EO59" version.
Source: OECD.

aims to reduce the replacement rate. An alternative would be to shift the financing of contributions to a broader base which would reduce the contribution rate. This option was explored extensively in the *OECD Jobs Study* (see OECD, 1995c). The majority of OECD countries already finance some social security from general revenues, *i.e.* a broader tax base than contributions based solely on earnings.

Considering a shift from labour taxes to general consumption taxes (*e.g.* VAT), the *OECD Jobs Study* noted that this would only be effective if the tax burden was shifted from those consuming out of labour income to those consuming out of capital or transfer income and concluded "a large shift towards taxing welfare recipients and lower income pensioners may lead to calls for increases in social benefits and public pensions which, if met, could seriously reduce the scope for tax cuts on labour". Indeed, in many countries indication of transfer payments would automatically undermine the effect of the shift. This illustrates that broadening the tax base to finance pensions reduces the consumption possible out of transfer incomes and so is equivalent to a cut in the value of transfers. Since earnings account for the great bulk of incomes (nearly 60 per cent on average in OECD countries), the degree to which capital and transfer incomes could bear taxes currently paid by labour is not large.

In addition, shifting the tax burden onto capital may also be counter-productive as capital accumulation improves labour productivity and so influences real wages. The results of "tax competition", the proliferation of special regimes and the degree to which international portfolio capital income escapes the tax net are contributing to an erosion of the capital income tax base. This would be accelerated by increases in the rate of tax on capital. Hence, shifting the burden onto capital may be neither desirable nor feasible.

As with general consumption taxes, shifting the tax burden onto energy would only have a positive overall effect if part of the tax burden was shifted onto those consuming out of capital or transfer income. The conclusion in the *OECD Jobs Study* was that "the most appropriate view of the effects of a shift from labour taxes to energy taxes is that they are likely to be small and of indeterminate sign".

In many countries it may be possible to broaden the base of social security contributions while maintaining the link with earnings. Table 5.4 shows that 11 OECD Member countries have an earnings ceiling on social security contributions, averaging around 155 per cent of average production worker earnings. Ceilings range from under 100 per cent in Turkey and just over 100 per cent in Canada to over 200 per cent in Luxembourg and the United States. Since 1985, ceilings have fallen relative to average production worker (APW) earnings in Austria, Germany, Spain and the United Kingdom, and have risen in the remaining countries. If ceilings are increased or removed, a lower contribution rate is required, but this may be counter-productive in systems with a strong actuarial link with benefits (since benefits will also be increased), unless the link is broken (see Chapter 2 for a discussion).

The scope for avoiding rises in social security contribution rates as the population ages is limited. In some countries, eliminating social security contribution ceilings would allow a lower rate as the earnings base is expanded. Shifting to a broader tax base would also allow a lower contribution rate. However, the scope for such a shift is limited by the fact that earnings are the dominant source of household income. Moreover, a shift to a tax

Table 5.4. **Structure of social security contributions, 1993**

	Base	Ceilings (% APW earnings)	
		Employee	Employer
United States[1]	Earnings	229	229
Japan	Earnings	–	–
Germany[1]	Earnings	169	169
France[1]	Earnings	131	131
Italy	Earnings	–	–
United Kingdom	Earnings	154	–
Canada[1]	Earnings	105	105
Austria	Earnings	146	146
Belgium	Earnings	–	–
Denmark	Earnings	–	–
Finland	Both	–	–
Greece	Earnings	212	212
Iceland	Income	–	–
Ireland[1]	Earnings	154	164
Luxembourg	Earnings	245	245
Mexico	Earnings	–	–
Netherlands[1]	Both	–	–
New Zealand	None	–	–
Norway	Earnings	–	–
Portugal	Earnings	–	–
Spain[1]	Earnings	219	219
Sweden[1]	Both	–	–
Switzerland[1]	Both	–	–
Turkey[1]	Earnings	83	–

''Both'' indicates that the social security system is financed in part on an income base and in part on an earnings base. Ceilings are presented as a percentage of the earnings of the average production worker. New Zealand has no social security contributions. Australia, Denmark and the Netherlands do not levy contributions on employers. Australia, which has no earnings-related scheme, is excluded from the table.
1. Indicates that the information refers to the pension scheme only; other countries' systems finance other forms of social insurance. The table refers only to earmarked social security contributions and does not take account of the financing of social spending from general revenues.
Source: OECD (1995*h*).

base that fully includes pensions is simply an implicit cut in pension benefits, although it may be desirable on equity grounds as pensioners may also have other taxable income.

D. Financial market implications of ageing populations

As discussed in Chapter 2, among the options under consideration in many countries are possible shifts from 1) public income support schemes to private schemes: 2) from unfunded to advance-funded pension schemes; and 3) from defined-benefit to defined-contribution schemes. Changes in the demographic profile of OECD countries and the reform of pension schemes may therefore exert important influences on the functioning of capital markets. Indeed, the reform of pension systems may contribute to the development and modernisation of financial markets. In particular, it may stimulate the modernisation of the financial infrastructure and the supply of risk capital. On the other hand, improvements in the functioning of capital markets and financial innovations may have a positive effect on the efficiency and the safety of the activities of pension funds and life insurance companies.

Stability is a central value in social security arrangements – especially pensions. Certainly, capital markets are inherently riskier than public finance in OECD countries. On the other hand, they offer the possibility of higher returns, free access to efficient capital markets as well as the use of professional investment strategies. Pension assets in the OECD area now total more than $6 trillion, an amount that may double by the year 2000 and continue to grow thereafter. This raises issues of competition among private operations, disclosure and transparency, external versus internal management, and rules that limit investment in equity or in foreign securities. For example, the share of foreign securities in these assets is small. Regulations will need to be reviewed if pension funds are to reap the diversification benefits that can be obtained by investing in the stock markets of the OECD countries and the emerging economies.

Shifts toward greater use of capital markets therefore will require careful review of regulatory and corporate governance regimes. Long-standing issues related to portability, vesting of pension rights, etc., may take on added importance. There would be increased urgency in having a broader range of savings/investment products available to the general public. The insurance sector, for example, could be called upon to participate on a wider scale in supplying the population with investment products. Countries considering an enlarged role for private pension schemes will have to consider the requirement for the prudential supervision of these schemes, as well as to reconsider their doctrines concerning risk and reward. Thus, a system that over-regulates pensions may under-perform in comparison with a system in which funds are allowed to formulate their own risk/reward strategies subject to prudential criteria.

E.   Ageing and saving

National saving consists of government saving and private saving. Both are influenced by ageing. The increased cost pressures on government that ageing creates were described above. Ageing, therefore, is a force toward government dissaving, one that will have to be offset by other means. It may also have adverse effects on private saving, although the story is not as straightforward.

Economists often think about private saving using a life-cycle framework. People are assumed to save during their working lives when household income is high and run down their savings during retirement. Savings should be low when workers are young and have children to support, should rise once the children have left home and, still later in the life-cycle, become negative when people retire.

This apparently simple model assumes, however, some sophisticated decision-making. First, people do not know how long they will live after retirement and therefore how much savings they will need. Second, the actual calculation of an optimal smoothing of life-cycle consumption is very difficult, even for experts. There are no good rules of thumb and learning by experience is impossible; we pass through the life-cycle only once. Third, savings require a degree of self-control and capacity to ''see far into the future'' that psychological studies suggest may be unrealistic.

Pensions help overcome these problems. They have the effect of reducing uncertainty about the length of retirement and removing the need to make difficult decisions about getting the best possible returns on savings. They provide a ''savings'' discipline. The precise role will depend on the type of pension. For example, as described in Chapter 4, decisions on the age at which people retire (or how much they save in preparation for retirement in addition to those pensions) are influenced, to some extent, by whether the pension is advanced funded or pay-as-you-go, or by the kind of actuarial adjustment made in cases of early retirement.

In reality, however, there is only mixed evidence in support of this traditional life-cycle model of private saving. The model predicts that people will accumulate sufficient assets to avoid a drop in standards of living on retirement, yet studies have shown that this is not the case. The model also implies that people will spend more than they earn once they reach retirement. Again, this is not always clear. There is some evidence that retired people continue to save, but at lower rates, although measured saving rates of old people may overstate their ''true savings'' as they do not take into account directly or indirectly (via bequests) paid services delivered by family members.

As another illustration, the life-cycle model predicts savings will grow if the number of people of working age is growing relative to the number of children and retirees. Savings should also grow in anticipation of longer periods of time spent in retirement. Yet the opposite has happened. In recent decades, the baby-boom generation has entered the labour force and there has been a reduction in fertility. The result has been an increase in the number of people of working age when compared to children and retirees. As well, the average length of retirement has increased yet private saving has tended to fall in most countries. There is some evidence, however, that the entry of the baby-boom generation into the labour force did in fact have positive effects on private saving but that other factors which reduced savings were more important, notably the slowdown in income growth. Hence, the future ageing of populations is likely to have adverse effects on private saving, although there is much uncertainty about the size of such effects.

There are different views about the effects of pay-as-you-go schemes on private saving. While some found a significant negative effect, others found both positive effects (as people retire earlier and therefore save more during their working life) and negative effects (as lifetime consumption increases as many people receive more in pension income than they have contributed) which are broadly offsetting.

For an economy as a whole, it is overall national saving – the sum of private and government saving – that matters for future economic growth. On balance, it seems likely that with ageing populations and unchanged policies, both private and government saving will fall in the future. But it is not strictly correct to simply add together separate

Illustrative saving scenario for OECD countries

The ageing of populations might have significant adverse effects on private saving. Applying the coefficient for the demographic effect on private saving as found by the IMF for industrial countries the increase in the dependency ratio of almost 20 percentage points leads to a decline in the average private saving rate of the OECD area by around 6 percentage points between 2000 and 2030. Among the major seven OECD countries the decline is particularly marked in Japan, Germany and Italy where the private saving rate would decline by 8 to 9 percentage points. If instead of the coefficient of the demographic effect on savings of –0.28, the lower coefficient of –0.16 is applied, the private saving rate in the OECD area would fall by more than 3 percentage points and in Japan, Germany and Italy by 4 to 5 percentage points.

The long-term scenario for government budgets developed by the Secretariat implies a significant adverse effect on government saving over the coming decades. With the assumption of unchanged policies (as compared with current legislated policies), government saving would fall by about 9 percentage points in Japan, by 15 to 20 percentage points of GDP (with base case assumptions about interest rate/growth differentials) and by 2030, there would be significant government dissaving in most OECD countries.

With the above illustrations for government saving and private saving, and assuming a 50 per cent Ricardian equivalence effect, national saving rates could decline between 2000 and 2030 by about 9 to 10 percentage points in the OECD as a whole. Most OECD countries could be left with extremely low net national saving and, in Italy, Austria, Denmark, Finland, the Netherlands and Sweden, national net saving would even become negative.

estimates of private and government saving because this ignores possible interactions between them. Views differ about the strength of these interactions. The strict Ricardian equivalence hypothesis[14] says that if government reduces its saving, households would know that they will have to pay higher taxes in the future and would immediately increase their savings. As a result, overall national saving would not be affected at all. Although most empirical studies reject full Ricardian equivalence, some interaction between government saving and private saving is likely,[15] especially in countries with adverse debt dynamics.

The illustrative saving scenarios under current policy settings are presented in Chart 5.2 for the OECD area; they suggest that the overall effect of ageing on national savings could be significant with the largest impact stemming from the sharp fall in government saving. However, macroeconomic models which are based on the theoretical framework of life-cycle saving and neo-classical growth theory show a much more significant fall in private saving[16] as well as national saving. These models provide a broader analytical framework, taking into account the inter-relationship between saving, investment and growth and, in some cases, also international repercussions. On the other

Chart 5.2. **Demographic impact on future net national savings in OECD countries**[1]

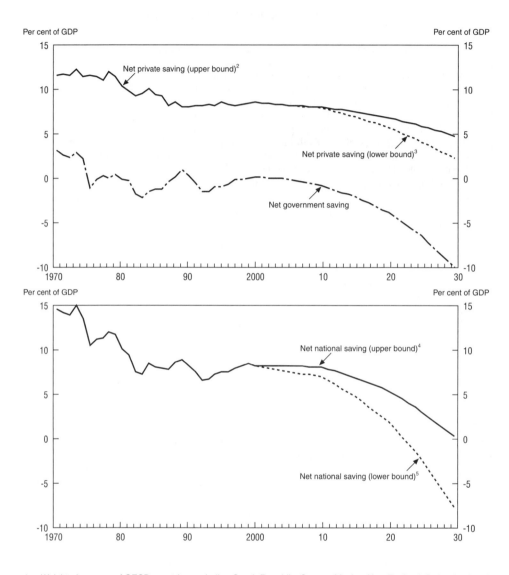

1. Weighted average of OECD countries excluding Czech Republic, Greece, Mexico, New Zealand, Switzerland and Turkey.
2. Applying the lower coefficient (-0.16) to the change in the dependency ratio.
3. Applying the higher coefficient (-0.28) to the change in the dependency ratio.
4. Applying the lower coefficient for the effect on private saving and assuming a 50 per cent Ricardian equivalence effect.
5. Applying the higher coefficient for the effect on private saving and assuming no Ricardian equivalence effect.

hand, they assume that economies are initially in equilibrium (with actual saving equal to optimal saving) which is unlikely to be the case.

Given these inconclusive results about the size of the demographic effects of ageing, caution is needed in drawing direct conclusions about the future development of national saving. More work is needed to examine these issues further and to consider the effects of ageing on private and national saving in OECD countries in a global framework that includes the projected demographic and economic developments in non-OECD countries.

Effects of lower saving on living standards

There are two opposing views on the effect of a demographically-induced fall in national saving on national well-being. One is the conventional view: that lower domestic savings leads to less productive investment, and that long run growth will be lower as a result. The other view argues that less investment will be needed because there are fewer workers to equip. Furthermore, saving and investment are not the only factors that determine long-term living standards. For example, the rate of growth of technical progress is more important; maintaining present rates in the future is likely to outweigh the adverse effects of ageing populations on living standards.[17] This debate cannot be resolved without more research into the long-run determinants of economic growth.

Nevertheless, provided higher savings are translated into greater wealth holdings, domestic or foreign, and these maintain their value, greater savings will provide more scope for dealing with the adverse effects of ageing. Policies aimed at higher national saving rates over the next few years are therefore prudent, and reducing government dissaving may be the most direct way of achieving that aim.

F. Conclusion: directions for reform

The ageing of the population will increase government spending, reduce revenues and increase government dissaving – and may also reduce national saving. There are a variety of ways in which the situation can be improved, but none are easy. These are discussed in detail above in Chapters 2 and 3, pensions and health.

Action is needed. Locking in an increasing proportion of national wealth to support increasing amounts of time in leisure near the end of life is simply bad social and economic policy. Failure to make needed changes, whatever the preferred path, will greatly restrict the freedom of coming generations to make their own decisions on how to spend national resources. Moreover, the sooner reforms are implemented, the less drastic the changes need be.

DEMOGRAPHICS

Population growth of OECD countries has been slowing in recent decades from 1.1 per cent per year in the 1960s to 0.8 per cent per year in the 1980s. For the 1990s a deceleration to 0.7 per cent is projected and during the first three decades a further deceleration to a rate of 0.2 per cent per year in the 2020s (Table A1). The total population of present OECD Member countries as a share of world population is projected to decline from almost 18 per cent in 1990 to about 13 per cent by 2030. Within the OECD area, there are some significant country differences. Only the United States, Canada, Australia, Iceland, Ireland, Mexico, New Zealand, Norway and Turkey are projected to continue to experience population growth after 2020. Even in these countries, the rate of growth is projected to slow significantly in the 2020s, to 0.4 per cent annually for the United States, 1.0 per cent for Mexico and 0.8 per cent for Turkey, three of the four most populous OECD countries. However, the population starts to fall in most of the other countries. In the decade ending 2010, the total population is projected to start to fall in Germany, Italy, Belgium, Portugal and Spain and the rate of shrinking is projected to accelerate over subsequent decades. In the decade ending 2020, the overall population starts to fall in Japan, Austria, Denmark and Greece. By the following decade, the population of Finland, Luxembourg, the Netherlands and Switzerland also starts to fall.

Working-age populations are projected to fall even faster. By the 2020s, working-age populations are falling everywhere except Ireland, Mexico and Turkey, and in twelve countries, including Germany and Italy, the working-age population is becoming smaller at a rate of more than $1/2$ per cent per year. The working-age populations of Japan, France, the United Kingdom and Canada are projected to shrink at slightly slower rates (roughly $1/2$ per cent) in the 2020s. By 2030, the working-age population of the OECD area will be $41/2$ per cent smaller than at its peak level in 2010, but in many countries the fall in working-age population from peak levels is much more pronounced – 24 per cent in Germany, 18 per cent in Italy, 17 per cent in Japan and 15 per cent in both the Netherlands and Spain.

Increasing dependency ratios

As working-age populations are shrinking faster than overall population, the share of population aged 65 and over (elderly share) and the ratio of those 65 years and over to the working-age population (elderly dependency ratios[18]) are growing and are projected to increase sharply after 2010. Between 1990 and 2030, the elderly share in the population for the OECD as a whole is projected to rise from just under 13 per cent to $221/2$ per cent, and the elderly dependency ratio is projected to rise from 19 per cent to 37 per cent – a near doubling of the elderly dependency rate within 40 years (Tables A2 and A3).

Table A1. Population indicators

	Total population (thousands)						Annual rates of change									
							Total population					Population aged 15 to 64 (working-age population)				
	1960	1990	2000	2010	2020	2030	1960-1990	1990-2000	2000-2010	2010-2020	2020-2030	1960-1990	1990-2000	2000-2010	2010-2020	2020-2030
United States	180 684	250 372	275 636	297 205	315 268	327 987	1.1	1.0	0.8	0.6	0.4	1.4	0.9	0.9	0.1	-0.3
Japan	93 260	123 537	126 840	127 946	126 026	122 154	0.9	0.3	0.1	-0.2	-0.3	1.2	0.0	-0.5	-0.8	-0.5
Germany[1]	55 433	79 452	81 097	78 867	76 393	73 495	0.4	0.2	-0.3	-0.3	-0.4	1.3	0.1	-0.5	-0.8	-1.5
France	45 684	56 735	59 425	60 993	62 121	62 661	0.7	0.5	0.3	0.2	0.1	0.9	0.4	0.4	-0.4	-0.4
Italy	48 967	57 661	57 930	56 824	55 139	53 172	0.5	0.0	-0.2	-0.3	-0.4	0.6	-0.1	-0.4	-0.8	-1.2
United Kingdom	52 599	57 411	58 882	59 568	60 315	60 570	0.3	0.3	0.1	0.1	0.0	0.3	0.2	0.2	-0.3	-0.6
Canada	17 870	26 522	29 841	32 166	34 019	35 001	1.3	1.2	0.8	0.6	0.3	1.8	1.1	0.8	0.0	-0.5
Australia	10 275	17 065	19 292	20 971	22 113	22 824	1.7	1.2	0.8	0.5	0.3	2.0	1.3	0.9	0.1	-0.3
Austria	7 048	7 712	8 138	8 180	8 169	8 093	0.3	0.5	0.1	0.0	-0.1	0.4	0.5	-0.1	-0.4	-1.0
Belgium	9 154	9 967	10 126	10 055	9 944	9 800	0.3	0.2	-0.1	-0.1	-0.1	0.4	0.0	0.0	-0.6	-0.9
Denmark	4 581	5 140	5 267	5 277	5 261	5 213	0.4	0.2	0.0	0.0	-0.1	0.6	0.2	-0.1	-0.5	-0.7
Finland	4 430	4 986	5 183	5 272	5 322	5 318	0.4	0.4	0.2	0.1	0.0	0.7	0.3	0.1	-0.7	-0.5
Greece	8 327	10 089	10 692	10 748	10 616	10 442	0.6	0.6	0.1	-0.1	-0.2	0.7	0.6	-0.1	-0.5	-0.7
Iceland	176	255	283	308	330	347	1.2	1.0	0.9	0.7	0.5	1.6	1.3	1.0	0.4	0.0
Ireland	2 834	3 503	3 723	4 019	4 262	4 460	0.7	0.6	0.8	0.6	0.5	0.9	1.4	0.7	0.5	0.3
Luxembourg	315	382	420	422	422	418	0.6	1.0	0.0	0.0	-0.1	0.7	0.8	0.0	-0.6	-0.9
Mexico	..	81 724	98 787	114 020	128 455	142 334	..	1.9	1.4	1.2	1.0	..	2.5	2.2	1.5	0.9
Netherlands	11 486	14 952	15 794	15 999	16 064	15 912	0.9	0.5	0.1	0.0	-0.1	1.3	0.3	0.1	-0.7	-1.0
New Zealand	..	3 363	3 679	3 920	4 135	4 300	..	0.9	0.6	0.5	0.4	..	0.8	0.7	0.2	0.0
Norway	3 585	4 242	4 443	4 547	4 650	4 726	0.6	0.5	0.2	0.2	0.2	0.6	0.5	0.4	-0.2	-0.4
Portugal	8 865	9 868	9 875	9 861	9 839	9 792	0.4	0.0	0.0	0.0	0.0	0.5	0.3	0.0	-0.2	-0.7
Spain	30 303	38 959	39 237	39 058	38 543	37 753	0.8	0.1	0.0	-0.1	-0.2	1.0	0.3	-0.2	-0.5	-1.0
Sweden	7 480	8 559	8 947	9 117	9 287	9 397	0.5	0.4	0.2	0.2	0.1	0.4	0.3	0.1	-0.2	-0.2
Switzerland	5 352	6 712	7 268	7 353	7 357	7 282	0.8	0.8	0.1	0.0	-0.1	0.9	0.6	-0.2	-0.5	-1.0
Turkey	27 755	56 098	66 130	74 897	83 442	90 761	2.4	1.7	1.3	1.1	0.8	2.7	2.2	2.0	1.1	0.7
Total OECD	636 463	935 266	1 006 935	1 057 593	1 097 492	1 124 212	0.9	0.7	0.5	0.4	0.2	1.1	0.7	0.5	0.0	-0.3
Total OECD[2]	581 030	770 727	823 372	860 786	888 509	904 083	0.9	0.7	0.4	0.3	0.2	1.2	0.6	0.4	-0.1	-0.4
World	3 019 000	5 266 007	6 113 680	6 944 433	7 742 124	8 474 017	1.9	1.5	1.3	1.1	0.9	..	1.7	1.6	1.2	0.8
OECD Europe	334 374	432 683	452 860	461 365	467 476	469 612	0.7	0.5	0.2	0.1	0.0	0.8	0.5	0.2	-0.2	-0.6

1. 1960 to 1990 west Germany, 1990 to 2030 total Germany.
2. Germany, Mexico and New Zealand excluded.
Source: Bos *et al.* (1994).

Table A2. Population sub-groups
In per cent of total population

	Population aged 65 and over (elderly share)						Population aged 0-14 and 65 and over						Population aged 75 and over				
	1960	1990	2000	2010	2020	2030	1960	1990	2000	2010	2020	2030	1990	2000	2010	2020	2030
United States	9.2	12.6	12.5	13.6	17.5	21.9	40.3	34.1	34.2	33.5	36.5	40.5	5.3	5.8	6.2	7.1	10.0
Japan	6.1	11.9	16.5	21.1	25.6	26.1	36.1	30.3	32.1	36.2	40.4	41.4	4.7	6.3	9.4	12.1	14.7
Germany	10.8	14.9	16.2	20.2	22.5	28.1	32.2	31.2	31.8	33.3	36.4	42.9	7.2	6.9	8.4	10.9	12.4
France	11.6	13.8	15.5	16.3	20.2	23.3	38.0	33.8	34.6	33.9	37.3	40.4	6.5	6.7	8.1	8.5	11.4
Italy	9.0	14.8	17.9	20.6	23.6	27.9	32.4	31.3	32.3	34.0	37.0	42.1	6.5	7.7	9.9	11.4	13.4
United Kingdom	11.7	15.7	15.9	17.0	19.7	23.0	34.9	34.6	35.1	34.4	36.8	40.5	6.8	7.3	7.9	8.8	10.6
Canada	7.6	11.3	12.3	13.8	18.2	23.1	41.3	32.2	32.6	32.2	36.0	40.8	4.5	5.3	6.2	7.3	10.3
Australia	8.5	10.7	11.3	12.6	16.3	20.3	38.7	32.9	32.4	32.3	34.9	38.5	4.1	4.8	5.3	6.4	8.9
Austria	12.2	15.1	15.6	18.3	20.8	25.7	34.3	32.5	33.0	33.9	36.2	41.6	7.1	7.2	8.3	10.1	11.6
Belgium	12.0	15.0	16.6	17.1	20.3	24.3	35.5	32.9	33.7	33.0	36.3	40.8	6.7	7.1	8.2	8.5	10.9
Denmark	10.6	15.4	14.5	16.4	20.1	22.6	35.8	32.4	32.9	33.9	36.7	40.1	6.7	6.6	6.6	8.3	10.4
Finland	7.3	13.3	14.4	16.2	21.3	24.1	37.7	32.6	33.0	33.5	38.5	41.5	5.6	6.2	7.3	8.4	12.1
Greece	8.1	14.2	17.1	19.0	21.2	24.6	34.2	33.2	32.8	34.1	36.4	39.9	6.4	6.7	9.3	10.1	11.8
Iceland	8.1	10.6	11.3	12.0	15.5	19.6	42.9	35.3	34.3	32.8	35.2	38.6	4.3	4.9	5.5	6.4	8.6
Ireland	10.9	11.4	11.2	11.9	14.2	16.4	41.4	38.1	33.3	33.9	34.5	35.3	4.6	4.9	5.1	5.9	7.4
Luxembourg	10.8	13.6	14.8	17.3	20.9	25.6	32.1	30.6	32.6	33.4	36.7	42.1	6.0	6.0	7.6	9.0	11.5
Mexico	..	3.7	4.3	5.3	7.2	10.0	..	41.7	38.1	33.4	31.3	32.5	1.3	1.3	1.8	2.4	3.5
Netherlands	9.0	13.2	14.1	16.4	21.5	26.0	39.0	30.8	33.2	32.2	36.7	42.3	5.6	6.3	7.2	8.8	12.1
New Zealand	..	11.1	11.3	12.6	15.9	18.9	..	33.7	34.2	33.4	35.4	38.1	4.4	4.8	5.2	6.3	8.3
Norway	10.9	16.3	15.5	15.8	19.7	23.0	36.8	35.2	35.1	34.1	36.9	40.6	7.0	7.9	7.7	8.3	11.2
Portugal	8.0	13.0	14.3	15.0	16.9	20.9	37.1	33.7	31.7	31.8	33.3	37.4	5.2	5.8	6.7	7.2	8.6
Spain	8.2	13.2	16.2	17.6	20.1	24.9	35.5	33.0	31.2	31.9	34.5	39.3	5.4	6.6	8.6	9.4	11.2
Sweden	11.8	17.8	17.0	18.4	21.6	23.1	34.1	35.6	36.7	36.9	39.4	41.3	7.9	8.7	8.6	9.9	12.1
Switzerland	10.3	15.0	15.8	19.1	23.3	27.5	34.0	31.6	33.2	34.9	38.4	43.5	7.1	7.2	8.7	11.0	13.6
Turkey	3.7	4.3	5.7	6.4	8.0	10.9	44.9	39.9	36.7	31.9	31.6	32.7	1.5	1.5	2.3	2.7	3.7
Total OECD	9.4	12.9	13.9	15.6	18.9	22.5	36.9	33.7	33.6	33.6	36.1	39.8	5.5	6.0	7.0	8.2	10.4
OECD Europe	9.7	13.7	14.7	16.4	19.5	23.2	36.5	33.6	33.5	33.6	36.3	40.2	6.0	6.4	7.5	8.6	10.8

Source: Bos *et al.* (1994).

101

Table A3. Dependency and support ratios

	Elderly dependency ratio[1]						Total dependency ratio[2]						Needs-weighted support ratio					
	1960	1990	2000	2010	2020	2030	1960	1990	2000	2010	2020	2030	1960	1990	2000	2010	2020	2030
United States	15.4	19.1	19.0	20.4	27.6	36.8	67.4	51.7	52.0	50.5	57.4	68.0	63.7	67.7	67.6	67.8	63.9	59.1
Japan	9.5	17.1	24.3	33.0	43.0	44.5	56.6	43.5	47.2	56.7	67.8	70.5	68.5	71.1	67.9	62.9	58.0	57.0
Germany	16.0	21.7	23.8	30.3	35.4	49.2	47.4	45.3	46.7	50.0	57.3	75.1	70.0	69.2	68.2	65.5	62.2	55.2
France	18.8	20.8	23.6	24.6	32.3	39.1	61.3	51.1	52.8	51.2	59.6	67.9	64.7	67.5	66.2	66.5	62.2	58.7
Italy	13.3	21.6	26.5	31.2	37.5	48.3	47.9	45.5	47.8	51.5	58.8	72.7	70.5	69.1	67.1	64.8	61.4	55.9
United Kingdom	17.9	24.0	24.4	25.8	31.2	38.7	53.7	52.9	54.0	52.3	58.3	68.0	67.3	66.1	65.6	65.8	62.8	58.7
Canada	13.0	16.7	18.2	20.4	28.4	39.1	70.5	47.5	48.3	47.5	56.3	69.0	63.3	69.7	69.1	68.8	64.0	58.4
Australia	13.9	16.0	16.7	18.6	25.1	33.0	63.2	48.9	48.0	47.6	53.7	62.6	65.3	69.4	69.6	69.2	65.6	61.2
Austria	18.6	22.4	23.3	27.7	32.6	44.0	52.1	48.2	49.3	51.3	56.7	71.4	67.7	68.0	67.4	65.7	63.0	57.0
Belgium	18.5	22.4	25.1	25.6	31.9	41.1	55.0	49.2	50.9	49.3	57.0	68.9	66.7	67.7	66.5	66.9	63.1	58.1
Denmark	16.5	22.7	21.6	24.9	31.7	37.7	55.8	47.9	49.1	51.3	57.9	67.0	67.0	68.0	67.9	66.4	62.8	59.2
Finland	11.7	19.7	21.5	24.3	34.7	41.1	60.6	48.4	49.2	50.4	62.7	70.9	66.6	68.6	67.9	66.8	60.9	57.6
Greece	12.3	21.2	25.5	28.8	33.3	40.9	52.0	49.6	48.8	51.7	57.1	66.3	69.3	67.9	67.0	65.3	62.7	58.7
Iceland	14.1	16.6	17.3	18.1	24.1	32.1	75.0	55.2	52.4	49.5	54.7	63.2	61.8	67.2	67.9	68.7	65.5	61.3
Ireland	18.6	18.4	16.7	18.0	21.7	25.3	70.6	61.4	49.8	51.3	52.6	54.5	62.1	64.8	68.9	68.1	66.8	65.3
Luxembourg	15.9	19.9	21.9	25.9	33.2	44.2	47.4	44.8	48.4	50.0	58.5	72.7	70.0	69.8	68.1	66.6	62.4	56.6
Mexico	:	6.4	7.0	8.0	10.4	14.8	:	71.6	61.5	50.2	45.5	48.1	:	64.5	67.5	71.2	72.2	70.1
Netherlands	14.7	19.1	20.8	24.2	33.9	45.1	63.9	44.5	47.7	47.5	58.1	73.2	64.9	70.2	68.6	67.8	62.3	56.3
New Zealand	:	16.7	17.1	18.9	24.6	30.5	:	50.9	51.9	50.2	54.7	61.6	:	68.6	68.1	68.2	65.4	62.1
Norway	17.3	25.2	23.9	24.0	31.2	38.7	58.2	54.4	54.1	51.7	58.6	68.3	66.1	65.3	65.7	66.5	62.8	58.7
Portugal	12.7	19.5	20.9	22.0	25.3	33.5	59.1	50.7	46.4	46.6	50.0	59.8	66.9	67.9	69.0	68.6	66.7	61.9
Spain	12.7	19.8	23.5	25.9	30.7	41.0	55.1	49.3	45.3	46.9	52.7	64.8	68.2	68.3	68.7	67.6	64.6	59.1
Sweden	17.8	27.6	26.9	29.1	35.6	39.4	51.8	55.3	57.9	58.5	65.1	70.4	68.0	64.5	63.9	63.2	60.1	58.0
Switzerland	15.5	22.0	23.6	29.4	37.8	48.6	51.5	46.1	49.6	53.7	62.4	77.0	68.7	68.8	67.2	64.6	60.4	54.9
Turkey	6.7	7.1	8.9	9.4	11.7	16.2	81.4	66.3	57.9	46.9	46.1	48.6	61.6	65.9	68.2	72.0	71.6	69.5
Total OECD	14.9	19.3	20.9	23.5	29.8	37.7	59.0	51.2	50.7	50.6	56.8	66.4	66.5	67.8	67.6	67.0	63.7	59.5
OECD Europe	15.3	20.6	22.1	24.7	30.8	39.2	57.9	50.9	50.4	50.6	57.1	67.4	66.7	67.6	67.4	66.7	63.4	59.0

1. Population aged 65 and over as a per cent of working age population.
2. Population aged 0-14 and 65 and over as a per cent of working age population.
Source: Bos *et al.* (1994).

Almost all OECD countries will be affected, but the increase is particularly sharp for Japan. In 1980, Japan had an elderly dependency ratio of 13½ per cent, the lowest in the OECD area apart from Mexico and Turkey. But by 2030, Japan's dependency ratio is projected to be one of the highest, more than tripling to reach 44½ per cent. Dependency ratios are also projected to exceed 40 per cent by 2030 in Germany, Italy and eight smaller countries and to be between 35 and 40 per cent in the United States, France, the United Kingdom, Canada and a further three smaller countries. These ageing population trends also reflect significant increases in the proportion of the population aged 75 and over. This proportion is projected to almost double for the OECD as a whole, from 5½ per cent in 1990 to 10½ per cent in 2030.

The increase in the elderly dependency ratio is often used as an indicator of the increase in the burden on the working-age population. However, an increase in the number of elderly dependent persons may be accompanied by a decline in the number of young dependent persons. This effect is reflected in the ratio of total dependent persons (children and elderly) to the working-age population (total dependency ratio). This ratio declined on average between 1960 and 1990 and will remain rather flat between 1990 and 2010, before rising again after 2010. It has been argued that the total dependency ratio may also be a misleading indicator of the effective burden of demographics on the working-age population as the resources spent on an elderly person and on a child may differ. To illustrate this for the United States, Cutler *et al.* (1990) have calculated a so-called needs-weighted support ratio which considers such differences. The support ratio is the ratio of the working-age population to the total (needs-weighted) population. The same weights[19] can be applied (as a first approximation) to calculate needs-weighted support ratios for other OECD countries.

All three indicators of the demographic burden on the working-age population point to the same general conclusion that the burden on the working-age population will increase significantly in the future. In Japan this increase is already underway, while in the United States it will be felt only after 2010. In Europe, the elderly dependency ratio starts to increase in the current decade, but the total burden on the working-age population as measured by the total dependency ratio or the needs-weighted support ratio shows a significant deterioration only after 2010.

Key assumptions underlying population projections

All population projections are driven by three key factors: fertility, life expectancy and migration. Fertility rates are already low in OECD countries – at, or below, replacement rates in all countries except Mexico and Turkey. Even in these two countries, fertility is projected to fall to replacement rates by 2010 and 2005, respectively. The United States, Iceland, New Zealand and Sweden all reach replacement rate in 1995 and fertility is assumed to remain at replacement rates. In those countries where fertility is currently below replacement rates, it is assumed to rise back to replacement rates by 2030. For Spain, which currently has the lowest fertility rate in the OECD, the rate is therefore assumed to almost double by 2030.

Life expectancy is also projected to increase by four to five years in all OECD countries, except for Mexico and Turkey, where life expectancy increases more rapidly, in part due to reductions in infant mortality rates. Estimated inward migration rates during the period 1990-1995 are largest in the United States, Canada and Australia, which also receive the largest absolute number of immigrants. Immigration rates are also relatively high in several European countries, including Germany, Austria, Greece and Switzerland. Only Ireland, Mexico and Portugal have net outward migration for the period 1990-1995. Migration rates in most countries are, however, projected to fall quite quickly, with only the United States, Canada and Australia projected to

103

Table A4. **Key demographic factors**

	Fertility rate[1]		Life expectancy at birth		Net migration rate[2]	
	1990-1995	2025-2030	1990-1995	2025-2030	1990-1995	2025-2030
United States	2.1	2.1	76.6	81.8	2.5	0.0
Japan	1.5	2.0	79.1	82.8	0.0	0.0
Germany	1.3	2.0	75.8	80.6	5.6	0.0
France	1.8	2.0	77.2	81.8	1.2	0.0
Italy	1.3	2.0	77.4	82.0	1.0	0.0
United Kingdom	1.8	2.0	76.2	81.0	0.9	0.0
Canada	1.9	2.1	77.8	82.2	4.4	0.0
Australia	1.9	2.1	76.7	81.0	5.7	0.0
Austria	1.6	2.0	76.6	81.5	5.1	0.0
Belgium	1.6	2.0	75.6	79.6	1.7	0.0
Denmark	1.8	2.0	74.7	79.1	1.9	0.0
Finland	1.9	2.1	75.4	80.8	1.6	0.0
Greece	1.4	2.0	77.4	81.7	6.8	0.0
Iceland	2.2	2.1	78.2	81.9	0.8	0.0
Ireland	2.0	2.1	75.2	80.6	–0.6	0.0
Luxembourg	1.7	2.0	75.7	80.6	10.2	0.0
Mexico	3.2	2.1	70.3	77.0	–2.3	0.0
Netherlands	1.6	2.0	77.3	81.5	2.6	0.0
New Zealand	2.1	2.1	75.7	80.5	1.2	0.0
Norway	1.9	2.1	77.2	81.7	1.9	0.0
Portugal	1.5	2.0	73.7	78.3	–0.8	0.0
Spain	1.2	2.0	76.8	81.2	0.5	0.0
Sweden	2.1	2.1	77.9	82.3	2.3	0.0
Switzerland	1.7	2.0	78.4	82.6	7.3	0.0
Turkey	2.9	2.1	67.3	74.8	0.0	0.0

1. Number of children per woman of childbearing age.
2. Number of net immigrants per 1 000 people.
Source: Bos *et al.* (1994).

continue receiving immigrants after 2010. By 2030, migration flows are assumed everywhere to be zero. Where immigration has been predominantly male, it is assumed that it is predominantly in the age group 15-30. However, where immigration has been more balanced between male and female, it is assumed that the immigrants are more widely distributed across age groups, including children and elderly.

The key demographic assumptions for OECD countries for fertility, life expectancy and migration that underpin the population projections (Bos *et al.*, 1994) used in this analysis are shown in Table A4.

NOTES

1. A more realistic picture is presented by Peter Scherer (1996) in "The Myth of the Demographic Imperative" (in Steurerle and Kawai) which shows the different responses by countries facing ageing pressures in the past – in programming directed to both older people and to the working age population.

2. Participation rates depend on social as well as economic factors making future trends difficult to predict. Sensitivity analysis indicates that the effects of increasing participation rates would be small.

3. Unless real earnings growth is so high that the effect of falls in numbers of contributors is counterbalanced. This is not now the experience of any OECD country.

4. In the latter case, the scheme will yield higher returns to contributions for high income participants than for low income participants, if contributions are related to earnings.

5. This may make older worker unemployment rates and incidence relatively higher (or lower) depending on how questions are answered in a labour force survey.

6. In 1990, only about 2 per cent of those aged 60-66 were in receipt of a partial pension in Denmark, and about 9 per cent of those aged 60-64 in Sweden.

7. For the major seven countries, see OECD Economics Department Working Paper 156, "Ageing Populations, Pension Systems and Government Budgets: How do they affect savings?" For other countries, see OECD Document ECO/CPE/WP1(96)5.

8. Pension contributions take into account announced changes in contribution rates.

9. Net debt is the difference between general government gross financial liabilities and gross financial assets.

10. For a fuller description of the interactions between primary balances, debt servicing costs and economic growth in the accumulation of public debt, see OECD (1995), *Economic Outlook*, No. 58.

11. Net debt servicing rates are calculated by dividing net interest payments by net debt.

12. Pensions often are linked to wages, which are linked to productivity growth – the main determinant of economic growth in these scenarios.

13. The contribution rate is calculated by multiplying the ratio of the average pension to the average wage by the ratio of the number of pensioners to the number of workers.

14. This is also sometimes referred to as the government debt neutrality hypothesis.

15. Some studies of industrial countries found that a unit government deficit increase (or drop in government saving) is offset by around a quarter or roughly half by an increase in private saving (Bosworth, 1993; Bernheim, 1987; Masson *et al.*, 1995), while others found evidence for full Ricardian equivalence (Seater, 1993).

16. See, for example, Auerbach *et al.*, 1989, Auerbach *et al.*, 1990; Hagemann and Nicoletti, 1989; Cutler *et al.*, 1990; Yoo, 1994.

17. Some argue that ageing slows technical progress as innovation is less profitable in shrinking markets for capital goods and as an ageing society loses ''dynamism'' (Simon, 1981; Wattenberg, 1987), while others find empirical evidence that innovation increases when labour gets scarce (Habakkuk, 1962; Cutler *et al.*, 1990).

18. Note that this standard definition rests on the assumption that the working-age population is 15-64, whereas the elderly dependency ratios for the major seven countries shown in the main text have taken the retirement ages in each country into account.

19. Cutler *et al.* consider age-specific use of private non-medical consumption, medical care and public education and attach an overall weight of 0.72 to the people under 20, of 1 to the people aged 20-64 and 1.27 to those aged 65 and over.

BIBLIOGRAPHY

ABEL-SMITH, B. (1996), "The escalation of health care costs. How did we get there?", in *Health Care Reform – The Will to Change*, OECD, Paris.

AKERLOF, G.A. (1991), "Procrastination and obedience", *AEA Papers and Proceedings*, Vol. 81, No. 2, May.

ALASTAIR, G. and P. FENN (1993), "Alzheimer's Disease: the burden of illness in England", *Health Trends*, Vol. 25, No. 1, pp. 31-37.

AUERBACH, A.J., J. CAI and L.J. KOTLIKOFF (1990), "US demographics and savings: predictions of three saving models", *NBER Working Paper*, No. 3404.

AUERBACH, A.J., L.J. KOTLIKOFF, R.P. HAGEMANN and G. NICOLETTI (1989), "The economic dynamics of an ageing population: the case of four OECD countries", *OECD Economic Studies,* No. 12 (later published as *NBER Working Paper,* No. 2797).

BARTEL, A.P. (1995), "Training, Wage Growth, and Job Performance: Evidence from a Company Database", *Journal of Labor Economics*, Vol. 13, No. 3.

BARTEL, A.P. and N. SICHERMAN (1993), "Technological Change and the Retirement Decisions of Older Workers", *Journal of Labor Economics*, Vol. 11, No. 1.

BERNHEIM, D. (1987), "Ricardian equivalence: an evaluation of theory and evidence", in S. Fischer (ed.), *NBER Macroeconomics Annual,* MIT Press, MA.

BLONDAL, S. and M. PEARSON (1995), "Unemployment and Other Non-Employment Benefits", *Oxford Review of Economic Policy*, Vol. 11, No. 1.

BLUNDELL, R.W. (1995), "The Impact of Taxation on Labour Force Participation and Labour Supply", *The OECD Jobs Study*, Working Papers No. 8, Paris.

BORSCH-SUPAN, A. and K. STAHL (1991), "Life cycle saving and consumption constraints. Theory, empirical evidence, and fiscal implications", *Journal of Population Economics*, No. 4.

BOS, E., M.T. VU, E. MASSIAH and R. BULATAO (1994), *World Population Projections, 1994-95*, The International Bank for Reconstruction and Development/The World Bank.

BOSHUIZEN, H.C. and H.P.A. van de WALTER (1994), *An International Comparison of Health Expectancies*, TNO Health Research, Leiden.

BOSWORTH, B. (1993), *Saving and Investment in a Global Economy*, The Brookings Institution, Washington.

CARROLL, C.D. and A. SAMWICK (1995), "The nature of precautionary wealth", *NBER Working Paper*, No. 5193, July.

CARROLL, C.D. and L. SUMMERS (1991), "Consumption growth parallels income growth: some new evidence", in B.D. Bernheim and J. Shoven (eds.), *National Saving and Economic Performance*, University of Chicago Press.

CUTLER, D.M., J.M. POTERBA, L.M. SHEINER and L.H. SUMMERS (1990), "An ageing society: opportunity or challenge?", *Brookings Papers on Economic Activity*, Vol. 1.

DILNOT, A. (1992), *Private Pensions and Public Policy*, OECD Social Policy Studies, No. 9, Paris.

EASTERLIN, R. (1980), *Birth and Fortune*, Basic Books, New York.

FELDSTEIN, M. (1974), "Social security, induced retirement, and aggregate capital accumulation", *Journal of Political Economy*, Vol. 82, No. 5.

FELDSTEIN, M. and C. HORIOKA (1980), "Domestic savings and international capital flows", The 1979 W.A. Mackintosh Lecture at Queen's University, *Economic Journal*, Vol. 90.

FRIES, J.F. (1980), "Ageing, natural death, and the compression of morbidity", *New England Journal of Medicine*, Vol. 330, pp. 130-135.

FRIES, J.F. (1989), "The compression of morbidity: near or far?", *Milbank Quarterly*, Vol. 67, pp. 208-232.

FUCHS, V. (1984), "Though much is taken – Reflection on aging, health and medical care", *Milbank Quarterly*, Vol. 62, No. 2, pp. 143-155.

FUCHS, V. (1990), "The health sector's share of the Gross National Product", *Science*, Vol. 247.

GALÍ, J. (1990), "Finite horizons, life-cycle savings, and time-series evidence on consumption", *Journal of Monetary Economics*, No. 26.

GRAHAM, J.W. (1987), "International differences in saving rates and the life cycle hypothesis", *European Economic Review*, Vol. 31, No. 8.

GURWITZ, J.H. (1994), "Erreurs de prescription chez les personnes âgées – La pointe de l'iceberg", *JAMA Édition française*, No. 279, October.

GUSTMAN, A.L., MITCHELL, O.S. and STEINMEIER, T. (1994), "The role of pensions in the labour market: a survey of the literature", *Industrial and Labor Relations Review*, Vol. 47, No. 3, April.

HABAKKUK, H.J. (1962), *American and British Technology in the Nineteenth Century*, Cambridge University Press.

HAGEMANN, R.P. and G. NICOLETTI (1989), "Population ageing: economic effects and some policy implications for financing public pensions", *OECD Economic Studies*, No. 12, Paris.

HAYASHI, F. (1992), "Explaining Japan's Saving: a review of recent literature", *Monetary and Economic Studies*, Bank of Japan, Vol. 10, November.

HORIOKA, C.Y. (1990), "Why is Japan's household saving rate so high? A literature survey", *Journal of the Japanese and International Economies*.

HORIOKA, C.Y. (1993), "Saving in Japan", in Arnold Heertje (ed.), *World Savings: an International Survey*, Blackwell, Cambridge.

HUBBARD, R.G., J. SKINNER and S.P. ZELDES (1994), "Expanding the life-cycle model: precautionary saving and public policy", *AEA Papers and Proceedings*, Vol. 84, No. 2, May.

HURD, M.D. (1990), "Research on the elderly: economic status, retirement, and consumption and saving", *Journal of Economic Literature*, Vol. 28, June.

INTERNATIONAL LEADERSHIP CENTER ON LONGEVITY AND SOCIETY (ILC) (1994), *An Economic Comparison of US and Japanese Systems of Health Care for the Elderly*, Japan.

KENNICKELL, A.B. (1990), "Demographics and household saving", *Monetary and Financial Studies*, Division of Research and Statistics, Board of Governors of the Federal Reserve System, April.

KOSKELA, E. and M. VIREN (1989), "International differences in saving rates and the life cycle hypothesis: a comment", *European Economic Review,* Vol. 33, No. 7.

LAZEAR, E. (1979), "Why Is There Mandatory Retirement?", *Journal of Political Economy,* Vol. 87, No. 6, December.

LEFF, N.H. (1969), "Dependency rates and savings rates", *American Economic Review,* Vol. 59.

LEIBFRITZ *et al.* (1995), *Ageing Populations, Pension Systems and Government Budgets: How Do They Affect Saving?,* Economics Department Working Paper No. 156, OECD, Paris.

LUMSDAINE, R.L. (1995), "Factors Affecting Labor Supply Decisions and Retirement Income", *NBER Working Paper,* No. 5223.

MASSON, P.R., T. BAYOUMI and HOSSEIN SAMIEI (1995), "Saving behavior in industrial and developing countries", *Staff Studies for the World Economic Outlook*, International Monetary Fund, September.

MASSON, P.R. and R.W. TYRON (1990), "Macroeconomic effects of projected population ageing in industrial countries", *IMF Staff Papers,* Vol. 37, No. 3.

McEVOY, G. and W. CASCIO (1989), "Cumulative evidence of the relationship between employee age and job performance", *Journal of Applied Psychology*, Vol. 74.

MEDOFF, J. and K. ABRAHAM (1980), "Experience, Performance and Earnings", *Quarterly Journal of Economics*, Vol. XCV, No. 4, December.

MINISTÈRE DU TRAVAIL (1994), *Travail, emploi, vieillissement*, La documentation française, Paris.

MISSOC (1995), *Social Protection in the Member States of the European Union*, Situation on 1 July 1994.

MODIGLIANI, F. and A. STERLING (1983), "Determinants of private saving with special reference to the role of social security – cross-country tests", in F. Modigliani and R. Hemming (eds.), *The Determinants of National Saving and Wealth,* St. Martin's Press, New York.

MUNELL, A.H. (1987), "The impact of public and private pension schemes on saving and capital formation", *Conjugating Public Private, The Case of Pensions*, No. 24, International Social Security Association, Geneva.

NICOLETTI, G. (1992), "Is tax-discounting stable over time?", *Oxford Bulletin of Economics and Statistics,* Vol. 54, No. 2.

OECD (1988*a*), *Aging Populations: The Social Policy Implications*, Paris.

OECD (1988*b*), *The Future of Social Protection*, Paris.

OECD (1991*a*), *Employment Outlook*, Paris.

OECD (1991*b*), *Shaping Structural Change: The Role of Women in the Economy*, Report by a high-level group of experts to the Secretary-General, Paris.

OECD (1992), *Employment Outlook*, Paris.

OECD (1993), *New Orientations for Social Policy*, Paris

OECD (1994*a*), *The Reform of Health Care systems, A Review of Seventeen OECD Countries*, Health Policy Studies No. 5, Paris

OECD (1994*b*), *The OECD Jobs Study*, Paris.

OECD (1994*c*), *The OECD Jobs Study: Part II The Adjustment Potential of the Labour Market*, Paris.

OECD (1995*a*), *The Transition from Work to Retirement*, Social Policy Studies No. 16, Paris.

OECD (1995*b*), *Employment Outlook*, Paris.

OECD (1995*c*), *The OECD Jobs Study: Taxation, Employment and Unemployment*, Paris.

OECD (1995*d*), "Industry by Occupation Data: Trends and Structural Shifts", Room Document 3, Paris.

OECD (1995*e*), *Social Transfers: Spending Patterns, Institutional Arrangements and Policy Reforms*, Paris.

OECD (1995*f*), *New Directions in Health Policy*, Health Policy Studies No. 7, Paris.

OECD (1995*g*), *Revenue Statistics of OECD Member Countries*, Paris.

OECD (1995*h*), *The Tax/Benefit Position of Employees*, Paris.

OECD (1996*a*), *Health Care Reform, The Will to Change*, Health Policy Studies No. 8, Paris.

OECD (1996*b*), *Lifelong Learning for All*, Paris.

OECD (1996*c*), *Technology, Productivity and Job Creation: Analytical Report*, Paris.

OECD (1996*d*) *OECD Health Data 1996*, Paris.

OECD (1996*e*), *Caring for Frail Elderly People – Policies in Evolution*, Social Policy Studies No. 19, Paris.

POTERBA, J.M., S.F. VENTI and D.A. WISE (1993), "Targeted retirement saving and the net worth of elderly Americans", *AEA Papers and Proceedings*, Vol. 84, No. 2.

POTERBA, J.M., S.F. VENTI and D.A. WISE (1995), "Do contributions crowd out other personal saving?", *Journal of Public Economics*, No. 58.

RABBIT, P. (1992), "Some issues in cognitive gerontology and their implication for social policy", in Heuvel *et al.* (ed.), *Opportunities and Challenges in an Ageing Society*, Amsterdam, North Holland.

ROBINE, J.M., M. BLANCHET and J.E. DOWD (eds.) (1992), *Espérance de Santé*, INSERM, Paris.

SEATER, J. (1993), "Ricardian equivalence", *Journal of Economic Literature*, Vol. 31, No. 1.

SCHERER, P.A. (1996), "The Myth of the Demographic Imperative", in C.E. Steuerle and M. Kawai (eds.), *The New World Fiscal Order, Implications for Industrialized Nations*, Urban Institute Press, Washington, DC.

SIMON, J.L. (1981), *The Ultimate Resource*, Princeton University Press.

STRAWCZYNSKI, M. (1993), "Income uncertainty and Ricardian equivalence", *The American Economic Review*, Vol. 85, No. 4, September.

TAYLOR, P. and A. WALKER (1995), "Combating Age Discrimination in Employment: Education versus legislation", *Policy Studies*, Vol. 16, No. 3, Autumn.

THALER, R.H. (1994), "Psychology and savings policies", *AEA Papers and Proceedings*, Vol. 84, No. 2, May.

van de WALTER, H.P.A. and R.J.M. PERENBOOM (eds.) (1995), *Policy Relevance and Conceptualisation*, Report of the first meeting of the Euro-REVES subcommittee, TNO Prevention and Health, Leiden.

WALTERS, W.E., E. HÄKKINEN, and A.S. DONTAS (1989), "Health, lifestyles and services for the elderly", *WHO: Public Health in Europe 29*, WHO, Copenhagen.

WARR, P. (1992), "Age and Employment", in Dunnette *et al.* (ed.), *Handbook of Industrial and Organizational Psychology*, Consulting Psychologists Press.

WATTENBERG, B.J. (1987), *The Birth Dearth,* Pharos Books, New York.

WHITTING, G. *et al.* (1995), "Employment policies and practices towards older workers: an international overview", *Employment Gazette*, April.

WHO (1989), *Health for the Elderly*, Report of a WHO Expert Committee, WHO technical Report Series 779, WHO, Geneva.

WHO (1995), *Epidemiology and Prevention of Cardiovascular Diseases in Elderly People*, WHO technical Report Series 853, WHO, Geneva.

WORLD BANK (1994), *Averting the Old Age Crisis: Policies to Protect the Old and Promote Growth*, A World Bank Policy Research Report, Oxford University Press.

YOO, P. (1994), "Boom or bust? The economic effects of the baby boom", *Federal Reserve Bank of St. Louis Working Paper*.

MAIN SALES OUTLETS OF OECD PUBLICATIONS
PRINCIPAUX POINTS DE VENTE DES PUBLICATIONS DE L'OCDE

AUSTRALIA – AUSTRALIE
D.A. Information Services
648 Whitehorse Road, P.O.B 163
Mitcham, Victoria 3132   Tel. (03) 9210.7777
Fax: (03) 9210.7788

AUSTRIA – AUTRICHE
Gerold & Co.
Graben 31
Wien I   Tel. (0222) 533.50.14
Fax: (0222) 512.47.31.29

BELGIUM – BELGIQUE
Jean De Lannoy
Avenue du Roi, Koningslaan 202
B-1060 Bruxelles
Tel. (02) 538.51.69/538.08.41
Fax: (02) 538.08.41

CANADA
Renouf Publishing Company Ltd.
1294 Algoma Road
Ottawa, ON K1B 3W8   Tel. (613) 741.4333
Fax: (613) 741.5439

Stores:
61 Sparks Street
Ottawa, ON K1P 5R1   Tel. (613) 238.8985

12 Adelaide Street West
Toronto, ON M5H 1L6   Tel. (416) 363.3171
Fax: (416)363.59.63

Les Éditions La Liberté Inc.
3020 Chemin Sainte-Foy
Sainte-Foy, PQ G1X 3V6 Tel. (418) 658.3763
Fax: (418) 658.3763

Federal Publications Inc.
165 University Avenue, Suite 701
Toronto, ON M5H 3B8   Tel. (416) 860.1611
Fax: (416) 860.1608

Les Publications Fédérales
1185 Université
Montréal, QC H3B 3A7   Tel. (514) 954.1633
Fax: (514) 954.1635

CHINA – CHINE
China National Publications Import
Export Corporation (CNPIEC)
16 Gongti E. Road, Chaoyang District
P.O. Box 88 or 50
Beijing 100704 PR   Tel. (01) 506.6688
Fax: (01) 506.3101

CHINESE TAIPEI – TAIPEI CHINOIS
Good Faith Worldwide Int'l. Co. Ltd.
9th Floor, No. 118, Sec. 2
Chung Hsiao E. Road
Taipei   Tel. (02) 391.7396/391.7397
Fax: (02) 394.9176

CZECH REPUBLIC – RÉPUBLIQUE TCHÈQUE
National Information Centre
NIS – prodejna
Konviktská 5
Praha 1 – 113 57   Tel. (02) 24.23.09.07
Fax: (02) 24.22.94.33
(*Contact* Ms Jana Pospisilova,
nkposp@dec.niz.cz)

DENMARK – DANEMARK
Munksgaard Book and Subscription Service
35, Nørre Søgade, P.O. Box 2148
DK-1016 København K   Tel. (33) 12.85.70
Fax: (33) 12.93.87

J. H. Schultz Information A/S,
Herstedvang 12,
DK – 2620 Albertslung   Tel. 43 63 23 00
Fax: 43 63 19 69
Internet: s-info@inet.uni-c.dk

EGYPT – ÉGYPTE
The Middle East Observer
41 Sherif Street
Cairo   Tel. 392.6919
Fax: 360-6804

FINLAND – FINLANDE
Akateeminen Kirjakauppa
Keskuskatu 1, P.O. Box 128
00100 Helsinki

Subscription Services/Agence d'abonnements :
P.O. Box 23
00371 Helsinki   Tel. (358 0) 121 4416
Fax: (358 0) 121.4450

FRANCE
OECD/OCDE
Mail Orders/Commandes par correspondance :
2, rue André-Pascal
75775 Paris Cedex 16 Tel. (33-1) 45.24.82.00
Fax: (33-1) 49.10.42.76
Telex: 640048 OCDE
Internet: Compte.PUBSINQ@oecd.org

Orders via Minitel, France only/
Commandes par Minitel, France exclusive-
ment :
36 15 OCDE

OECD Bookshop/Librairie de l'OCDE :
33, rue Octave-Feuillet
75016 Paris   Tél. (33-1) 45.24.81.81
(33-1) 45.24.81.67

Dawson
B.P. 40
91121 Palaiseau Cedex   Tel. 69.10.47.00
Fax: 64.54.83.26

Documentation Française
29, quai Voltaire
75007 Paris   Tel. 40.15.70.00

Economica
49, rue Héricart
75015 Paris   Tel. 45.75.05.67
Fax: 40.58.15.70

Gibert Jeune (Droit-Économie)
6, place Saint-Michel
75006 Paris   Tel. 43.25.91.19

Librairie du Commerce International
10, avenue d'Iéna
75016 Paris   Tel. 40.73.34.60

Librairie Dunod
Université Paris-Dauphine
Place du Maréchal-de-Lattre-de-Tassigny
75016 Paris   Tel. 44.05.40.13

Librairie Lavoisier
11, rue Lavoisier
75008 Paris   Tel. 42.65.39.95

Librairie des Sciences Politiques
30, rue Saint-Guillaume
75007 Paris   Tel. 45.48.36.02

P.U.F.
49, boulevard Saint-Michel
75005 Paris   Tel. 43.25.83.40

Librairie de l'Université
12a, rue Nazareth
13100 Aix-en-Provence Tel. (16) 42.26.18.08

Documentation Française
165, rue Garibaldi
69003 Lyon   Tel. (16) 78.63.32.23

Librairie Decitre
29, place Bellecour
69002 Lyon   Tel. (16) 72.40.54.54

Librairie Sauramps
Le Triangle
34967 Montpellier Cedex 2
Tel. (16) 67.58.85.15
Fax: (16) 67.58.27.36

A la Sorbonne Actual
23, rue de l'Hôtel-des-Postes
06000 Nice   Tel. (16) 93.13.77.75
Fax: (16) 93.80.75.69

GERMANY – ALLEMAGNE
OECD Bonn Centre
August-Bebel-Allee 6
D-53175 Bonn   Tel. (0228) 959.120
Fax: (0228) 959.12.17

GREECE – GRÈCE
Librairie Kauffmann
Stadiou 28
10564 Athens   Tel. (01) 32.55.321
Fax: (01) 32.30.320

HONG-KONG
Swindon Book Co. Ltd.
Astoria Bldg. 3F
34 Ashley Road, Tsimshatsui
Kowloon, Hong Kong   Tel. 2376.2062
Fax: 2376.0685

HUNGARY – HONGRIE
Euro Info Service
Margitsziget, Európa Ház
1138 Budapest   Tel. (1) 111.62.16
Fax: (1) 111.60.61

ICELAND – ISLANDE
Mál Mog Menning
Laugavegi 18, Pósthólf 392
121 Reykjavik   Tel. (1) 552.4240
Fax: (1) 562.3523

INDIA – INDE
Oxford Book and Stationery Co.
Scindia House
New Delhi 110001   Tel. (11) 331.5896/5308
Fax: (11) 371.8275

17 Park Street
Calcutta 700016   Tel. 240832

INDONESIA – INDONÉSIE
Pdii-Lipi
P.O. Box 4298
Jakarta 12042   Tel. (21) 573.34.67
Fax: (21) 573.34.67

IRELAND – IRLANDE
Government Supplies Agency
Publications Section
4/5 Harcourt Road
Dublin 2   Tel. 661.31.11
Fax: 475.27.60

ISRAEL – ISRAËL
Praedicta
5 Shatner Street
P.O. Box 34030
Jerusalem 91430   Tel. (2) 52.84.90/1/2
Fax: (2) 52.84.93

R.O.Y. International
P.O. Box 13056
Tel Aviv 61130   Tel. (3) 546 1423
Fax: (3) 546 1442

Palestinian Authority/Middle East:
INDEX Information Services
P.O.B. 19502
Jerusalem   Tel. (2) 27.12.19
Fax: (2) 27.16.34

ITALY – ITALIE
Libreria Commissionaria Sansoni
Via Duca di Calabria 1/1
50125 Firenze   Tel. (055) 64.54.15
Fax: (055) 64.12.57

Via Bartolini 29
20155 Milano   Tel. (02) 36.50.83

Editrice e Libreria Herder
Piazza Montecitorio 120
00186 Roma   Tel. 679.46.28
Fax: 678.47.51